Neil ec Tremblay

March 4, 2013

# Cedar Lake Park Association

# Cedar Lake Park Association

## A History

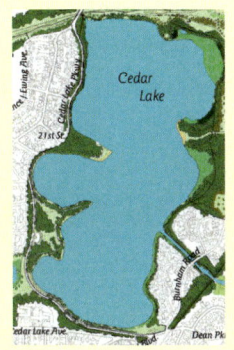

## Neil Trembley

### for the
**CEDAR LAKE PARK ASSOCIATION**

The story of citizens' action in the creation and development
of an urban nature park and regional commuter trail
in Minneapolis, Minnesota

*This publication has been financed in part with funds provided by the State of Minnesota from the Arts and Cultural Heritage Fund through the Minnesota Historical Society.*

Published by the Cedar Lake Park Association

This publication was made possible in part by the people of Minnesota through a grant funded by an appropriation to the Minnesota Historical Society from the Minnesota Arts and Cultural Heritage Fund. Any views, findings, opinions, conclusions or recommendations expressed in this publication are those of the author and do not necessarily represent those of the State of Minnesota, the Minnesota Historical Society, or the Minnesota Historic Resources Advisory Committee.

COVER AND BOOK DESIGN: Judy Gilats
COVER ILLUSTRATION: Frederick Appell, *Cedar Lake Park—Minneapolis.* 1991.
BACK COVER PHOTOGRAPH: Meredith Montgomery, *Looking west from the Kenwood Park trailhead.* 2010.
FRONTISPIECE PHOTOGRAPH: Meredith Montgomery, *Cedar Lake Park looking east toward downtown Minneapolis.* Fall 2005.

*To Doris*

# Contents

**FIGURE 1.** Map of Cedar Lake and surrounding area, 2011. Image courtesy of CLPA.

# Preface

ON APRIL 20, 1989, SIXTY-FIVE CITIZEN ACTIVISTS FROM MINNE-apolis, Minnesota, founded an organization called Save Cedar Lake Park (SCLP). Its goal was to create a rustic nature park out of an abandoned railroad yard on the north end of Cedar Lake in Minneapolis. Over the next two years, SCLP enlisted over two thousand members and raised $1.6 million in public funds and private donations. By the end of 1991, forty-eight acres of land originally slated for private development had become a public park.

SCLP led a drive to develop a trail on the park's edge. It raised $500,000 in private funds for the trail's construction. By 1995, the Cedar Lake Regional Trail stretched from Highway 100 in St. Louis Park to the edge of downtown Minneapolis.

In 2000, the group—renamed the Cedar Lake Park Association (CLPA)—began an eleven-year campaign to extend the Cedar Lake Regional Trail to the Mississippi River through the heart of downtown Minneapolis. CLPA's efforts have been a significant factor in making Minneapolis the number one Bicycle City in the United States.

The CLPA name seldom appears in official documents. A 1991 land acquisition agreement records that the Minneapolis Park & Recreation Board (MPRB) acquired the forty-eight acres and created a park with the help of funding provided by the state. Minnesota Department of Transportation construction documents from 1995 indicate that the Minneapolis Department of Public Works (MPW) constructed the Cedar Lake Regional Trail with federal and state funding. Although some recognition of CLPA's role in completing the trail to the Mississippi River can be found intermittently, the documents do not tell the whole story.

### Documenting the Cedar Lake Park Story

Chronicling the founding of Save Cedar Lake Park became more important as time passed and memories faded. Unless documented, the accomplishments of private citizens' groups are often forgotten. (A noted local newspaper columnist told the group that he could find no record of CLPA's role in creating Cedar Lake Park.) The initial purpose for commissioning this book was to document the founding of Save Cedar Lake Park and its role in creating an urban nature park and regional commuter trail.

As the project progressed it became clear that the story could have value to those outside the group; the association's philosophy and organizational structure could provide a guideline for other citizen groups to accomplish their objectives. Moreover, the Cedar Lake Park story demonstrates how citizens' groups can partner with public agencies to get projects accomplished. Perhaps this book can serve as a primer for how citizen-activist groups can affect change in the twenty-first century.

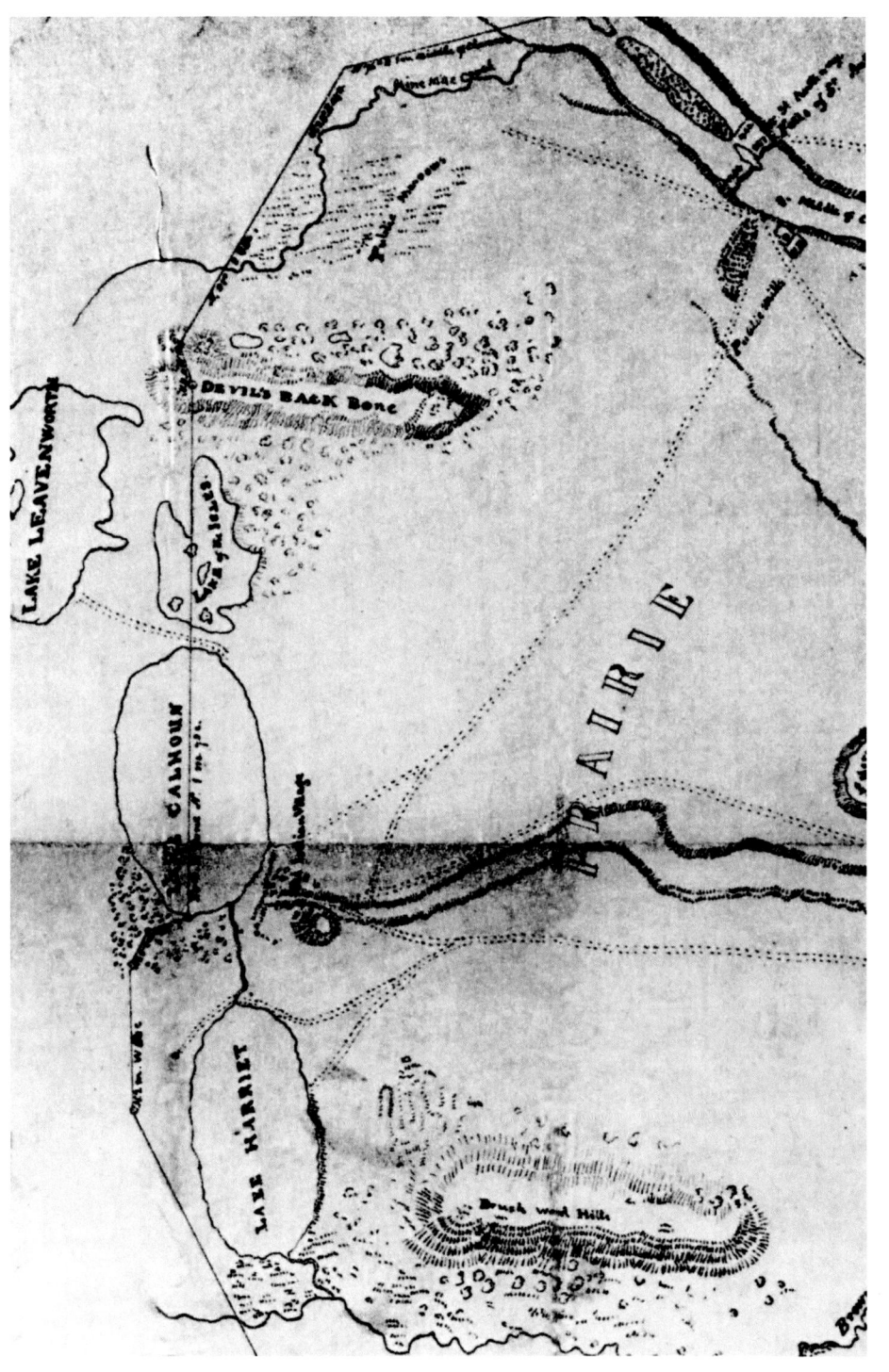

**FIGURE 2.** *Map of Fort Snelling Military Reserve, 1839.* James L. Thompson, Minnesota Historical Society, St. Paul.

# Abbreviations

| | |
|---|---|
| BMNA | Bryn Mawr Neighborhood Association |
| BN | Burlington Northern Railroad |
| BNSF | Burlington Northern Santa Fe Railway |
| CAC | Citizens' Advisory Committee |
| CLPA | Cedar Lake Park Association |
| DNR | Minnesota Department of Natural Resources |
| DRC | Data Recognition Corporation |
| FHWA | Federal Highway Administration |
| GN | Great Northern Railway |
| HCRRA | Hennepin County Regional Railroad Authority |
| KIAA | Kenwood-Isles Area Association |
| M&StL | Minneapolis & St. Louis Railroad |
| MnDOT | Minnesota Department of Transportation |
| MPRB | Minneapolis Park & Recreation Board, also known as Park Board |
| MPW | Minneapolis Department of Public Works, also known as Public Works |
| SCLP | Save Cedar Lake Park |
| SHPO | Minnesota State Historic Preservation Office |
| SP&P | St. Paul & Pacific Railroad |
| StPM&M | St. Paul, Minneapolis, and Manitoba Railway |

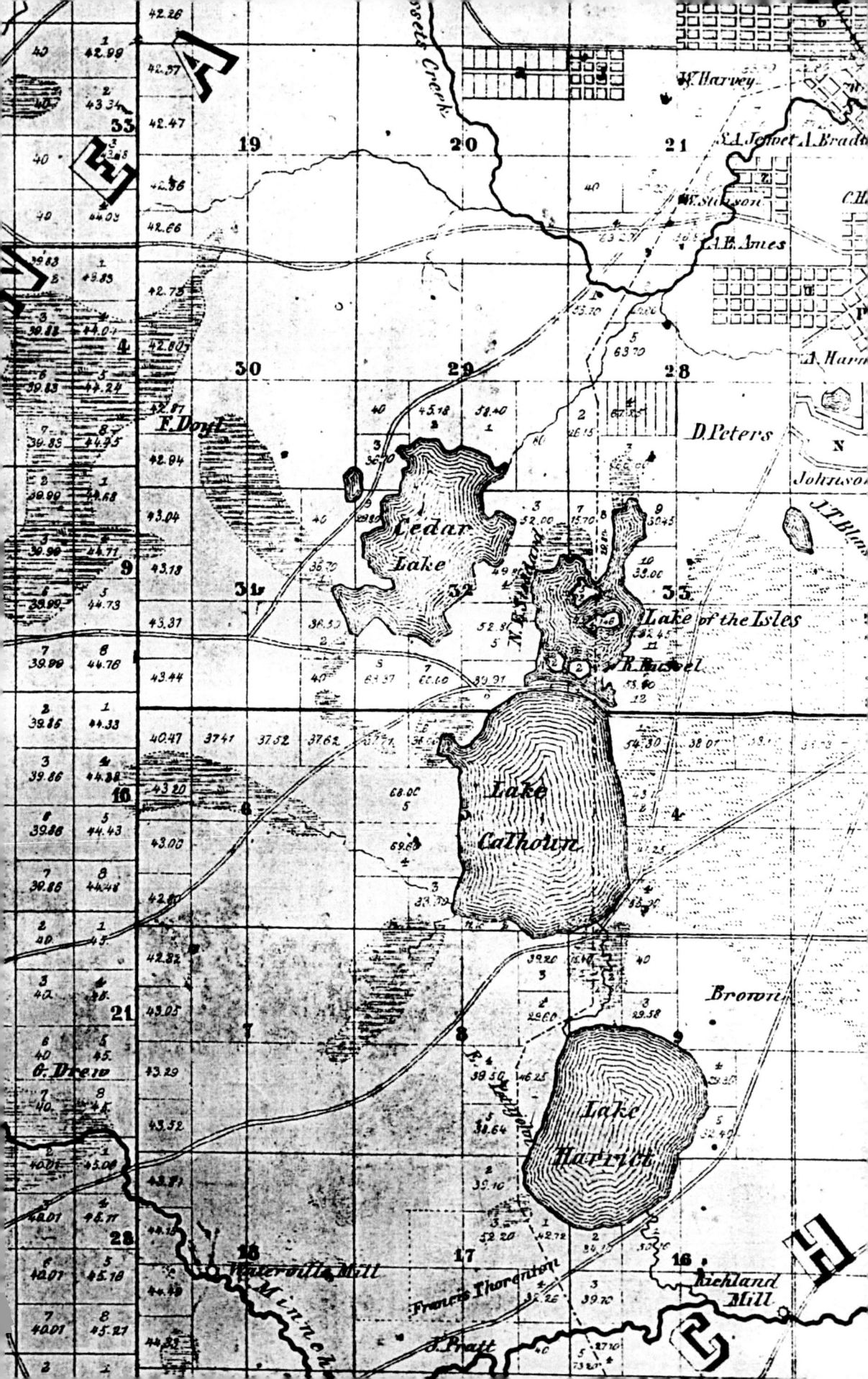

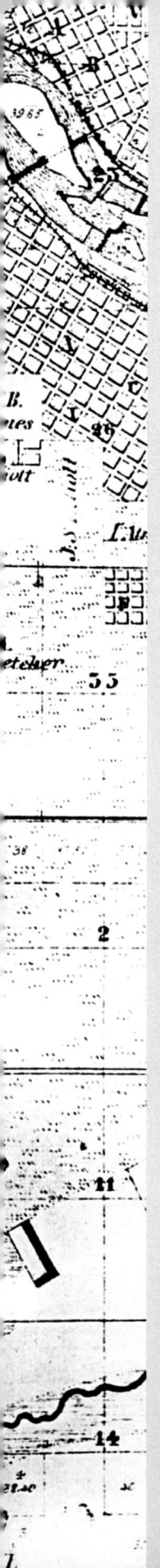

**FIGURE 3.** *Hennepin County, Hennepin County Map 1860.* DETAIL. Hennepin County Library, James K. Hosmer Special Collections Library, Minneapolis Collection.

**FIGURE 4.** *Hennepin County, Hennepin County Map 1860.* DETAIL. Hennepin County Library, James K. Hosmer Special Collections Library, Minneapolis Collection.

# Introduction:
# The Land and Its Early Uses

### Creating Cedar Lake

PRIOR TO THE LAST ICE AGE, THE MISSISSIPPI RIVER RAN WEST OF its present course through Minneapolis, Minnesota. The pre-glacial river carved a deep valley through the area that now comprises Cedar Lake, Lake of the Isles, Lake Calhoun, and Lake Harriet.[1] During the last ice age about 12,000 years ago, the retreating glacier deposited huge chunks of ice in the ancient river valley and filled the rest of it with glacial drift. Over the course of time, the ice melted and formed a chain of lakes. Atop the chain sat Cedar Lake.

### Pre-European Settlement

The people who inhabited the area just prior to European settlement in the nineteenth century were the Yankton branch of the Dakota nation. They and their traditional enemies, the Ojibwe to the north, often skirmished in the area. The zone of conflict ran from the Ojibwe strongholds on the Rum River to the Dakota settlements on the Minnesota River.[2] Cloudman's Village, founded in 1828 on the southeast shore of Lake Calhoun in Minneapolis, was "on the Dakota-Ojibwe frontier."[3] Cedar Lake appears to have been within the zone dividing the two nations.

No records exist of Native American settlements at Cedar Lake. Perhaps the tension between the Ojibwe and Dakota or the marshlands that surrounded Cedar Lake made it undesirable. An early map (see *figure 2*) shows a path between Lake Calhoun and Cedar

1

Lake; apparently it had been visited regularly—perhaps by hunting or fishing parties.

## Mapping the Area

Fort Snelling Commander Joseph Plympton commissioned one of the first maps of the Minneapolis area in 1839 (see *figure 2*). On it, Cedar Lake is marked Lake Leavenworth, after the first commander of the fort. A large moraine called "Devil's Backbone" is indicated where Lowry Hill is today. The map shows a footpath running from the north shore of Lake Calhoun to the southeast shore of Cedar Lake. An island appears on the west side of Cedar Lake and bays jut out on the east side.[4]

In 1853, the federal government opened the west side of the Mississippi to settlement. That same year it commissioned a land survey of the area. According to Assistant Surveyor Jesse T. Jarrett's field notes, the soil around Cedar Lake was second rate (i.e., unsuitable for farming). On the east side of the lake, Jarrett found linden, aspen, elm, and black oak trees along with an undergrowth of oak thickets. West of the lake, he noted a large tamarack swamp. Northeast of the lake, the surveyor found some ironwood and elm trees. He also recorded a small stream running northeast from the lake to Bassett's Creek. The area around Cedar Lake was not promising for settlement; while it did have some timber that could be logged, it did not contain any arable land.[5]

## Commercial Uses

By the second half of the nineteenth century, the area around Cedar Lake had developed into a transportation hub. By 1860, a wagon trail ran west from Minneapolis along the northwest corner of the lake; it was called Cedar Lake Road (see *figure 3*). Stagecoaches used the road to transport settlers and cargo out to the new towns springing up near Lake Minnetonka. Within a decade, however, commercial activity along the road declined as a new form of transportation made its mark on the Cedar Lake area.

In 1867, crews from the St. Paul & Pacific Railroad (SP&P) began laying a track from downtown Minneapolis to the west, following the old low-lying, pre-glacial riverbed. When they reached Cedar Lake, SP&P engineers altered the course. Instead of continuing west, they turned to the south and built an earthen causeway through the east bay of the lake. Once beyond the southern tip of the lake, the line resumed its western course out to Lake Minnetonka. (Eventually this railroad, albeit under a different name and owner, would reach the Pacific Ocean.) Where the tracks rounded the southeast corner of the lake, a station was built. From there, guests would ride by boat to the Oak Grove Hotel, a resort built in the 1870s at the southwest end of the lake. Like the necessity to transport visitors by water to the hotel, the need to alter the rail line course appears to confirm the marshy and impassable state of the land at that time.

In 1883, soon after James J. Hill took control of the SP&P,* work crews laid tracks through the north end of Cedar Lake (see *figure 5*). By 1912, more than thirty sets of tracks filled the space between Cedar Lake and the Bryn Mawr bluffs. The industrial character of the area remained largely unchanged until the 1970s. The Burlington Northern Railroad, as it was known by then, controlled the north end of Cedar Lake.

In 1871, owners of the rival Minneapolis & St. Louis Railroad (M&StL) also laid tracks on the east side of Cedar Lake. Soon after, the M&StL erected wooden buildings near the northeast corner of the lake, the first step in creating an extensive railway repair and maintenance complex within the corridor. In addition, they erected an ornamental train station at 21st Street and Upton Avenue. Nearby residents of the new "suburb" of Kenwood used the cupola-shaped Kenwood Depot to commute into the city.

The proximity of the M&StL to Cedar Lake spurred another commercial activity. In the 1890s, the lake was known for the clarity and purity of its water. Ice harvesting became a big business. A photo-

---

*Shortly after James J. Hill took control of the St. Paul & Pacific, he renamed it the St. Paul, Minneapolis, and Manitoba. Around the turn of the century it became the Great Northern, and later the Burlington Northern. In 1996, it became the Burlington Northern Santa Fe Railway. Today it's the BNSF Railway.

graph taken around that time shows workers from Cedar Lake Ice Company loading ice blocks from the lake directly onto a train car. Around 1900, workers erected a huge icehouse on the east shore of the lake. The railroad built a siding to the icehouse so that blocks could be loaded into specially built cars. Shipments traveled as far south as Saint Louis, where the ice was used to cool drinks in fashionable restaurants. The giant icehouse burned down in a spectacular blaze in 1918 and was never rebuilt.

It seems there was at least one other "commercial" activity on the east side of Cedar Lake at that time. Theodore Wirth wrote of "a resort established on the east shore called 'Stetson's Cedar Lake Park'. . . . This was a rather gay place in its time, and can be remembered by many for the lively episodes that occurred there, which sometime were recounted in the newspapers."[6] Stetson's Cedar Lake Park was a bordello.

### Recreational and Residential Uses

By the late 1800s, the large east bay of Cedar Lake had become a recreational Mecca. Working-class families from the city took the train to the Kenwood Depot and spent their weekends boating on the lake or fishing along its shoreline. By 1895, they could overnight at the brand-new Hotel Kenwood, just one block east of the station. The east side of Cedar Lake had become both a commercial and a recreational area.

To connect Cedar Lake to Lake of the Isles, the Minneapolis Park Board in 1913 lowered Cedar Lake by five feet. As the waterline receded, Cedar Lake's east bay dried. Recreational use declined and the east side of the lake became a backwater. The area was held in such disregard that in the 1950s and 60s, the city of Minneapolis used the old, dried-up east bay as a garbage dump. Eventually the earth covered over the garbage and a hilly cottonwood forest arose. The lake's eastern shore acquired a reputation as a wild and even dangerous place, attracting a certain element who liked the isolation the forest provided.

Paradoxically, the east side of Cedar Lake was also home to a very affluent residential neighborhood. By the late 1800s, a cluster of houses crowded the lake's southeastern shoreline. When the U.S. surveyor general tried to push the homeowners off the lake in 1901, the residents sued the federal government. The homes were allowed to remain along the lakeshore. (Cedar Lake is the only lake in the city of Minneapolis that has private homes abutting its shoreline.) Although the Minneapolis Park Board did eventually establish a legal right to the shoreline, this residential enclave made it next to impossible to develop a pathway along the eastern side of the lake. In 1913, the Park Board dug a canal from Lake of the Isles to the southeast shore of Cedar Lake, further isolating the area.

### Parkland

As park historian David C. Smith noted in his survey of Minneapolis parks, "No lake in the Minneapolis park system was considered for acquisition as a park for so long and took so long to acquire as Cedar Lake."[7] The Park Board first began acquiring acreage around Cedar Lake in 1905. The Park Board's main interest at that time was to build a road along the southern and western shores as part of the Grand Rounds—a belt of parkways designed to encircle the city. The Park Board began buying up parcels of land around the lake and by 1968 it owned the entire shoreline; however, railroad activity to the north and east of the lake effectively blocked further park expansion.

The combination of these commercial, recreational, and residential activities effectively blocked the northern and eastern shores from development typical of most Minneapolis lakes. Cedar Lake was unique.

**FIGURE 5.** *Great Northern Railroad tracks on north edge of Cedar Lake going west.* Circa 1900. William Wallof, Hennepin County Library, James K. Hosmer Special Collections Library, Minneapolis Collection, Wallof Collection, W081.

# 1
## Starting a Movement

O NE A PRIL EVENING IN 1989, A GROUP MET IN AN OFFICE BUILDING
on a bluff overlooking Cedar Lake in Minneapolis, Minnesota. Most
of the group came from neighborhoods surrounding the lake. They
gathered to discuss a wedge of land on the north end of Cedar Lake.
It was a former rail yard. It was a once and future place with an unusual history.

### Altering the Lake

In 1860, Cedar Lake was considerably larger and its shape much different than it is today (see *figure 4*). To the southwest, a shallow bay
extended to what is now France Avenue. Louise Island stood off the
western shore. On the east, a large bay reached present-day Thomas
Avenue. To the north, the lake lapped up against the base of the
Bryn Mawr bluff.

Starting in 1867, the contour of the lake began to be altered. That
year officials at the St. Paul & Pacific Railroad ordered their crews to
build an earthen causeway through the east bay of Cedar Lake. This
split the bay in two.

In 1883, railroad magnate James J. Hill (who had taken over
the SP&P) had a double track mainline constructed on a causeway
through the northern part of Cedar Lake (see *figure 5*). Hill was com-
peting with the M&StL to capture the luxury resort business on the
shores of Lake Minnetonka. This shorter, straighter route—called
the "Minnetonka Cutoff"—allowed Hill to boast the fastest line to
the lake.

In 1903, newspaper articles reported concern over the fallen water level of Cedar Lake. Local residents claimed the lake had gone

7

down seven feet over the previous decade.[8] Some locals blamed ice harvesting for the fall in the lake level, while others noted the previous decade had been the hottest and driest on record. In 1913, the lake was lowered five feet to connect it to Lake of the Isles. The depressed lake level uncovered a large swath of land below the Bryn Mawr Bluff. Taking advantage of this, James J. Hill used sand from the top of the bluff and mixed in locomotive hotbox cinders to fill in the area between the north shore of Cedar Lake and the base of the Bryn Mawr Bluff. Once the land was stabilized, Hill's engineers laid out an extensive rail yard.

The owners of the M&StL also took advantage of the lowered lake by using cinder and sand to fill in the east bay and build an extensive rail facility. On the west side of the lake, the Minneapolis Park Board connected Louise Island to the mainland and created Cedar Point peninsula. The bay on the southwest end of the lake also dried up and became a little-used open space. By the end of the twentieth century, it was almost impossible to recognize the original contour of the lake (compare *figure 1* and *figure 4*). Not since the retreat of the last glaciers 12,000 years before had the area been so thoroughly reshaped.

### Consolidation and Transformation

By the 1950s, switching yards and maintenance facilities crammed the area between the lake and the bluffs to the north and northeast. The railroads barred access to this part of the lake. Guard dogs roamed the grounds and locals trespassed at their peril.

The second half of the twentieth century saw a series of takeovers and consolidations that slowly began to change the character of Cedar Lake. Due to the merger of James J. Hill's old rail empire into the Burlington Northern Railroad (BN) in 1970, the rail yard on the north shore of the lake became redundant and was closed. BN knocked down its shops and tore up the tracks. Only BN's single-track main line remained intact.

In 1960, the Chicago and North Western Railway acquired the M&StL. The Cedar Lake Yards became redundant and were closed in 1984. The Chicago and North Western sold its holdings on the northeast side of the lake to the Hennepin County Regional Railroad Authority (HCRRA). By 1986, the extensive complex of shops on the northeast corner of the lake was reduced to rubble and only a single track remained along the east side of Cedar Lake.[9] Suddenly, a considerable amount of space opened around Cedar Lake.

Nature abhors a vacuum. Where iron tracks once bound the earth, grasses and wildflowers now rose up. Birds came to nest and foxes made dens. Deer began to nibble on the fresh green plants. Although trains still traversed the area—and remnants of roads, docks, and shops still scarred it—the land quickly reverted to a makeshift prairie. Soon, locals began to venture into it.

### Finding Value in the Land

Runners soon beat a path through the area. One jogger noted early one morning, "Around one of the bends in the tracks, you could see the skyline of Minneapolis. It was just breathtaking to watch the sun come up. It was golden. But something was going to happen to the land. It wasn't going to stay this way forever."

Others began exploring the area. Trekking through the old rail yard, a few began to glimpse its potential. Though some feared it as a dangerous place, many loved its wild and natural beauty. During walks, some visitors started to pick up trash accumulating in the area. One local placed trash cans in strategic locations. Each barrel displayed the slogan *Nurture Nature*. Soon the barrels were overflowing. "It was a squatter's strategy," he explained, "to encourage people to begin using the land as a park, regardless of ownership: to begin to see the park as a fait accompli."

Developers eyed the area as well, noting the desirability of this wedge of land less than a mile from downtown Minneapolis. In the fall of 1988, BN put forty-eight acres of land north of Cedar Lake up for sale. Surveyors' stakes suddenly dotted the prairie. Within a few weeks, the neighbors around Cedar Lake received notice of a public meeting to discuss the future of the abandoned railroad yard on the north end of the lake.

The city council person chairing the meeting that evening began by discussing how quickly a buyer could be found. When one citizen suggested converting the land to a park, the chair person turned the discussion to road access. It became apparent to attendees that the city council had already decided on residential development.

## WHICH DO YOU WANT?

HOUSING FOR FEW?

OR PARKS FOR ALL?

## Save Cedar Lake Park

an association for the preservation of Cedar Lake Park has been working very hard to preserve the open areas north, northeast, and northwest of Cedar Lake.

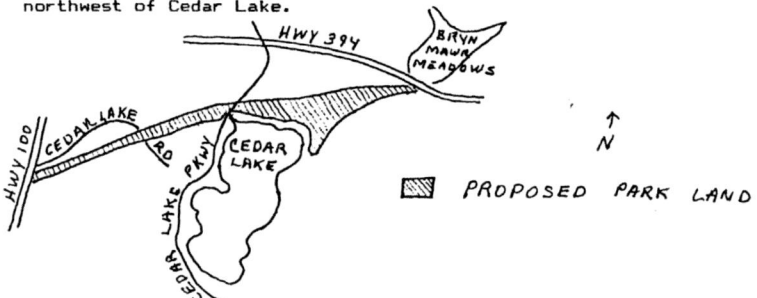

We are working with the City Council, Metro Council, Mpls. Foundation, Nature Conservancy, neighborhood organizations, Park Board, State Legislators and Glacier Park Co., a subsidiery of Burlington Northern Railroad and have made substantial progress. In 1991, we will be raising acquisition funds, but

**WE NEED YOUR IMMEDIATE HELP:**
SCLP's operating funds are very low. Without a loan from a member of the steering committee we could not have printed our last newsletter. We need operating funds to continue our efforts. Please dig deep into your gift-giving pocket and help us by making a contribution to SAVE CEDAR LAKE PARK. This year the Parks Dept. is 108 years old; and it acquired Cedar Lake 82 years ago. In commemoration, consider donating $108 or $82. Your contribution may be tax-deductible.

**FIGURE 6.** Save Cedar Lake Park Flyer. Image courtesy of CLPA.

### Creating a Vision

Several people who attended that first meeting did not like what they had heard. *Cedar Lake is unique,* they thought. *It doesn't feel like the other city lakes. It's wild and natural. Building houses along the north shore would destroy that aesthetic.* As they shared their concerns about the future of the land, they decided that something had to be done—and quickly; so they started to call their neighbors.

Soon a core group emerged that was committed to creating a park out of the old rail yard. They sought to fashion a message that would rally support for the idea. They came up with a simple but powerful message. "WHICH DO YOU WANT?" their first flyer asked, "HOUSING FOR FEW? OR PARKS FOR ALL?" (See *figure 6.*) They went door-to-door, inviting neighbors to a second meeting, where a very different vision of the land's future would be discussed.

Sixty-five citizens gathered on that April evening in 1989. The knocking on doors and handing out of flyers had paid off. The group had tapped a wellspring of public interest. Many who came were intrigued by the idea of converting the abandoned railroad yard into a public park.

The core group had prepared well for the meeting. "In the beginning, many of the people were asking, 'what's going to happen to the land?'" one attendee reminisced. "We decided to frame the question as 'What *should* happen? What is the best use of this land?'" Asking that basic question changed the tone of the debate and sparked new ideas. Participants became stakeholders. A way forward emerged, along with a slogan: "Who doesn't love a park?"

The participants realized that just being against residential development was self-defeating. They decided not to *oppose,* but to *propose.* They left the meeting with an alternative to private development. They chose a name* that described their goal: "Save Cedar Lake Park."

---

*Save Cedar Lake Park formally incorporated in 1989 as the *Cedar Lake Park Preservation and Development Association,* a 501(c) (3) non-profit organization.

# 2

# Building an Organization

CEDAR LAKE IS UNIQUE. ALTHOUGH A LINK IN THE MINNEAPOLIS Chain of Lakes, Cedar Lake is unlike her sister lakes. The history of commercial, recreational, and residential activity around the northern and eastern shoreline has effectively blocked access to much of the lake and makes walking around its shoreline a daunting task.*

Locals gave names to certain features—Hidden Beach, Indian Mound, and Bum's Ridge—that evoked its wild qualities. Despite the lake's close proximity to downtown Minneapolis, it felt remote. Any time of the day, one could wander its woodlands in solitude. Walled off by rail tracks with no streets bisecting it and no parking lots adjacent to it, the area was difficult to access. For many, the isolated area had become a place of respite.

Save Cedar Lake Park sought to create a plan that embraced the area's wild nature while reflecting a progressive urban aesthetic. The prevailing urban park landscape design—manicured turf, a smattering of trees, asphalt walkways—often resulted in a barren landscape that could not support a wide diversity of plants and animals. Such a landscape was also dependent on costly doses of fertilizers, pesticides, and fossil fuels for constant mowing. Since plants and animals had already begun to reclaim the old rail yard, SCLP sought to encourage what had taken hold to support a greater diversity of flora and fauna. They envisioned a place where human intervention would be minimal, a place without playground equipment or a rec-

*While the north and east shores are still wild and difficult to access, the development of the Cedar Lake Parkway in the early part of the 1900s make the south and west shores of the lake easily accessible, and that side is much more like the rest of the Chain of Lakes.

reation center. They wanted to create a nature conservancy in the heart of a metropolis.

### Adding a Linear Park

Some members considered that the park must not only be *established*, it must also be *connected*. They advocated paved bicycle and pedestrian trails that would wind through the park.

Linear parks, like the Minnehaha Parkway, had taught Minneapolis residents that greenways could connect the city's lakes and rivers, as well as soften the hard edges of urban life. From all over the Twin Cities, people came to enjoy the system of linked parkways that nearly encircled the city, the Grand Rounds National Scenic Byway (known by most locals as the "Grand Rounds"). Conceived in the late nineteenth century by legendary landscape architect Horace W. S. Cleveland,[10] the Grand Rounds was developed in the early twentieth century by noted Minneapolis Park's Superintendent Theodore Wirth.[11] Almost a century later, Save Cedar Lake Park proposed a green corridor that would run from Cedar Lake through the center of downtown Minneapolis and tie the Chain of Lakes to the Mississippi River—a distance of 4.5 miles. Such a trail would create a non-motorized transportation belt stretching across the city. Subsequent spurs could link the city to the suburbs and help unite its disparate parts. For some members, the park and the trail became intertwined.

Not surprisingly, tension developed between park lovers and trail enthusiasts. Part of the park's allure, the park lovers argued, was its inaccessibility; its remoteness made it all the more unique and precious. They perceived the park as a refuge and envisioned the area as a place to commune with nature. To them, a paved trail was anathema to the concept of a nature park. They advocated wood-chipped nature paths and gravel trails. In the ensuing discussions, many heatedly advocated this position.

Others began to see the virtue in creating trails that would bring the metropolitan communities closer together. Park-starved neighborhoods, they argued, would see the creation of Cedar Lake Park as just one more goodie for the rich folk in Kenwood. But a trail that connected to their neighborhoods would make the park a valuable *regional* asset, available to everyone.

In its twenty-two year history, no other issue provoked such heated discussion. Ultimately the group reached consensus: protection and connection. To assuage those concerned that the trail would overwhelm the park, members vowed to conserve as much of the core area as possible by pushing the trail to its outer edge. While the debate had threatened to tear the group apart, achieving consensus on this critical issue bonded the group closer together and created its central narrative.

### Defining and Organizing the Vision

On June 19, 1989, SCLP officials signed the Articles of Incorporation. Article II stated that the specific aims and purposes of this corporation shall be:

1. To promote the acquisition for public parkland . . . along the north and northeast sides of Cedar Lake in Minneapolis.
2. To study the environment of this presently undeveloped land and determine ways to preserve or enhance its wildlife capabilities, its qualities as a natural and open space, and its potential as a public park.
3. To educate and inform the public . . . on the existence of this open space and its potential as an addition to the park system.
4. To study and promote the linking of this area near Cedar Lake with parks and other parts of Minneapolis or its suburbs through bikeways, trails and walking paths.
5. To promote the establishment of parklands and public paths on land owned by Hennepin County, formerly Chicago North Western Railroad land, which is contiguous to the Cedar Lake/ Burlington Northern property.

The fifth point proposed creating parkland out of property owned by the HCRRA on the east side of Cedar Lake. (The HCRRA had purchased the Chicago North Western land for potential light rail use.) Although SCLP did not have the means to pursue this goal, it wanted to stake out and claim the land. Even at this early date, SCLP was embracing the idea of a "Greater Cedar Lake Park."*

———

In July of 1989, SCLP began discussing organizational issues. Out of these discussions came guidelines that would enable SCLP to function effectively. (For a full list of SCLP Organizational Guidelines, see Appendix A.) Although all had value, some of the guidelines become fundamental to SCLP's success:

1. **CREATE THE VISION.** Be bold. Base the vision on values and needs. Be positive. Be for something rather than against something.

2. **DEFINE THE VISION IN BROAD TERMS.** Avoid specific design details. Don't get bogged down in minutiae. The devil is in the details.

3. **CLAIM, NAME, AND SAVE** the land for the highest and best use. This may take some daring, such as strategically placing garbage cans throughout the park and speaking of the park as if it already existed, but boldness often pays dividends.

4. **WORK THROUGH IDEAS AND PLANS UNTIL THERE IS CONSENSUS.** Present a united front. Be of one mind, especially in front of other stakeholders. This is an arduous task and it often involves compromise, but never on core values. The power of a group lies in articulating a unified vision.

Notice that these four guidelines are all framed in the positive. While the group came together because it didn't want residential development on a piece of land, it started its drive with a fully articulated concept that advocated protecting and developing the land as green space.

Once you've created and defined the vision and outlined the project, you can move forward to the next steps:

---

*On the east side and north end of Cedar Lake, a pie-shaped park area stretches from the Kenwood Bluff on the east to the Bryn Mawr Bluff on the north. This bluff-to-bluff area is often referred to as Greater Cedar Lake Park.

With its incorporation, SCLP began discussing the means to communicate its vision to the public and to define itself in a way that spoke to the most basic desires of the urban citizenry. Out of those early sessions came the following statement.

# MISSION STATEMENT

### SAVE CEDAR LAKE PARK'S MISSION IS TO:

- Establish a rustic nature park on the north and northeast shores of Cedar Lake and along the railroad right-of-way from Cedar Lake to Highway 100. This urban wildlife and nature preserve would be unique among big-city parks in the United States.
- Link together the Chain of Lakes, the Mississippi Riverfront Park, and the western Minneapolis suburbs by a green-way—a corridor of foot and bike paths.
- Complete the vision of the 1883 grand design of the Minneapolis Park Board.
- Generate citizen and public involvement in the development of paths and connecting trails, thereby fostering a new sense of community in our urban environment.

The statement went beyond land acquisition and trail construction to embrace the city's history and connection to communities. Later, SCLP refined its mission statement to include educational opportunities in the park and community outreach, but its core mission remains intact.

5. **COMMUNICATE THE VISION, THE VALUES AND THE NEED.** Make your ideas the basis for discussion, the groundwork for further action, and the common vocabulary about the project.

6. **HANG IN THERE!** These projects are always long, drawn-out affairs, taking much more time and energy than anyone imagines at the start. Stick with it and don't get worn down. Go walk the area to remind yourself of what you are striving for. Have small celebrations to restore enthusiasm and ensure the staying power of the group. Make it fun!

These guidelines proved so successful that in 1994, the Minnesota Department of Natural Resources distributed SCLP's Organizational Guidelines to user groups across the state.[12]

### Laying the Groundwork

To save Cedar Lake Park, the group needed time to rally support and raise funds to buy the land. Burlington Northern, on the contrary, wanted a quick sale of its asset. Save Cedar Lake Park needed to assure the railroad that, given time, it had the ability to pull together a deal. A few members of SCLP used their own money to travel to BN's headquarters in Fort Worth, Texas, and discuss the issue with executives there. The railroad agreed to withhold the forty-eight acres of property from the market while SCLP sought funding. SCLP had created a little breathing space.

Before it could even begin negotiations, SCLP needed to establish the land's worth. Luckily, one of its members was a developer, and he volunteered to give an estimate of the value of the land. After a quick survey, he placed its value at between $1.6 and $2 million. Now the group had a baseline. Later negotiations set the price of the land at $1.7 million, so the original estimate was fairly accurate.

SCLP contacted the Minneapolis Park & Recreation Board (MPRB). Park Board Superintendent David Fisher and his assistant Al Whitman immediately realized the area's potential. By June of 1989, the MPRB convened the Cedar Lake Park & Trail Citizens' Advisory Committee (CAC) to develop a plan. Meanwhile, the Park

Board commissioned landscape architect Theodore J. Wirth, the grandson and namesake of Minneapolis Park's renowned superintendent, to produce a feasibility study for "a nature park with connecting trails."[13] By the end of 1989, Wirth's study concluded that the idea was feasible and desirable.

The Park Board made sure that SCLP was well represented on the CAC; it also chose SCLP's president to be the citizen leader of the CAC. Out of this decision a unique partnership began developing between MPRB and SCLP.

The Park Board faced serious challenges in funding its vast park system. During the 1980s, it had embarked on an ambitious plan to build additional recreational facilities in the inner city; it also spent funds acquiring expensive strips of land along the Mississippi River. MPRB knew that any public funds procured for Cedar Lake Park would exclude maintenance costs, which would fall on MPRB's shoulders. Yet the Park Board saw the value of the property north of Cedar Lake, both as a park and as a connecting greenway.* The Park Board enthusiastically embraced the project.

MPRB could provide no funding of its own. Funds might be available from the Minnesota Legislature, but state grants would require a local match. The Park Board challenged SCLP to raise the money.

### Going to the People

Although it was tempting, SCLP resisted approaching elected officials immediately for funds. As one member explained, "We tend to think that elected officials can do more than they can actually do. Elected officials can only do what the people want them to do. We decided that our appeal had to be to the people first. Those officials who were true leaders and could see the value of the project would be grateful and would lead. Those who did not see the value of it immediately would follow once we had sufficient numbers of people

---

*In this, SCLP visionaries had been prescient. Had SCLP pushed for the park only, the MPRB might have passed on the property. The trail connections made this piece of land far more desirable.

supporting the idea. We also wanted it to be apolitical. We didn't want it to become identified with X or Y politician, one party or the other. We wanted people to say *yes* to the nature park because it appealed to their deepest values." For the money needed to acquire the land, SCLP appealed to the citizenry first.

### Planning a Campaign

Group members began the task of raising $533,000—one-third of the purchase price for the land. They attended planning meetings, raised working capital, wrote editorials, drafted grant proposals, organized fundraisers, and made presentations to rally support. To keep in touch with its members, it began to publish a newsletter (see *figure 7*).

### Attracting Members

The group discussed how to structure membership. While most groups charged dues, SCLP decided on a different approach. To show a broad base of support for its mission, SCLP wanted as many people as possible on its membership rolls. SCLP decided that membership would be free and open to anyone. Setting up at venues like the Minneapolis Uptown Art Fair, they started gathering signatures. According to the appeal on the sign-up sheets, qualification for membership in SCLP was "an interest in preserving land on the north and northeast shores of Cedar Lake as a nature park and connecting this park with trails to the Chain of Lakes, Mississippi Riverfront and other Regional Parks."

Soon SCLP had over 2,000 members from across the region. Instead of demanding dues, SCLP asked for donations. Hundreds of small contributions poured in. These were vital for defraying the cost of the fundraising campaign. The impressive membership roll would also convince elected officials that SCLP was a serious player. Showing a broad base of support for the project also gave SCLP leverage with potential wealthy donors.

# Save Cedar Lake Park

## UPDATE—DECEMBER 1989

The last two months have been very busy! The Citizens Committee working with Ted Wirth completed its concept design work and presented it to the Planning Committee of the Park Board on November 15th. **The major points of the Wirth Plan are:**

1) the land at the north and northeast shores of Cedar Lake to be a nature park,

2) a foot and bike path corridor be developed along the existing railroad tracks connecting the Chain of Lakes and the River Front (this path corridor could also be extended west to Lake Minnetonka, the Loos Line Trail and Baker Park in the western part of Hennepin County), and

3) the Bassett Creek be developed as a park with trails to connect Wirth Park with the Chain of Lakes/River Front Corridor.

The Park Board's Planning Committee voted to accept the plan and recommend it to the full Board. A good number of persons who served on the Citizens Committee are also members of **Save Cedar Lake Park** (SCLP). Randall Bradley, the chair of the Citizens Committee and a member of SCLP, took the lead role in presenting the plan to the Planning Committee of the Park Board. Several other SCLP members who also served on the Citizens Committee spoke in favor of the plan.

The Wirth Plan was also presented to the Metropolitan Council's Parks and Open Space Commission on November 21st. The main presenters of the plan were Ben Wright, Dan Dailey and Brian Willette—all from SCLP. Many others spoke in favor of the plan, including:

- **Cliff French**, former Superintendent of the Regional Park system, who said that the Wirth Plan should be the top priority of the regional park system;
- **Pat Scott**, Minneapolis Councilperson-elect, who stressed the need to seize opportunity now to make a major contribution to the Minneapolis and regional park systems;
- **Walter Carpenter**, former Minneapolis Park Board Chair, who emphasized the unique opportunity which now exists and may never come again to have a nature park within walking distance of downtown Minneapolis and have a connecting corridor with

trails between the River and the Chain of Lakes; and

- A representative from **Don Fraser**'s office who said the Mayor is fully behind this project.

The Minneapolis Park Board is in the process of taking the next step. It is preparing a special request to be submitted to the Metropolitan Council for additional monies (most likely, two million) to start the land purchasing process. If the request is accepted, the Met Council will make it a part of its larger request to the State Legislature for funding. This process needs monitoring and special attention by SCLP. Working with the Met Council and the State Legislature will be both challenging and exciting! All SCLP members may be asked to become involved in the next steps are taken. We will try to keep you informed. Please be ready to help!

In addition to working with the various governmental bodies, SCLP is addressing other issues. SCLP always needs and welcomes new members. Join the effort to recruit new members. See the other side of this news letter for details. We are also asking all members to consider a holiday gift to help **Save Cedar Lake Park**. The more $$$ the more merrier! Give what you can! $10, $25, $50, $100, $250, $500, $1,000, or more!

With your continued support, Cedar Lake Nature Park with its connecting trail corridor between the River Front and the Chain of Lakes will become a reality.

### Have a Wonderful Holiday Season!

---

The Steering Committee continues to meet weekly. The Committee is considering calling a late January or early February meeting of the membership to present the:

**Wirth Plan for Cedar Lake Park and Connecting Trail Corridor**

&

**'90 Goals for Save Cedar Lake Park**

Date, Time and Place to be announced!

---

**FIGURE 7.** First edition, *Save Cedar Lake Park Update*. Image courtesy of CLPA.

**Creating Campaign Tools**

When members approached people to sign up they often were asked, "Where is Cedar Lake Park?" At the outset of the campaign, most Minneapolis park-goers couldn't pick out the old rail yard on a city map, much less see its potential as a nature park.

To show the site's importance as a critical link in the larger Minneapolis chain of greenways, a local artist created the first map of Cedar Lake Park. Members also wrote press releases and submitted editorials to local newspapers, pointing out the new park's location and its potential for enhancing the metropolitan trail system.[14]

Campaigns need visual hooks. One member created an impressive one: a 20-foot-high thermometer on the Ewing Avenue curve just south of the Cedar Lake Parkway Bridge. In giant red letters,

**Save Cedar Lake Park**

Save Cedar Lake Park (SCLP) invites you to a meeting on Wednesday, October 24, to learn more about Cedar Lake Nature Park and the connecting trail corridor. Cedar Lake Nature Park is located on the northern shore of Cedar Lake and is connected via the corridor to the Mississippi Riverfront Park, Nicollet Island, the Chain of Lakes, Wirth Park, western Hennepin County and western suburbs.

This is a unique opportunity for you to see a slide presentation of the Nature Park and trail corridor as well as SCLP's maps and drawings of area plans. SCLP will also discuss the current state of negotiations for the purchase of the park land.

Please come and show your support for Cedar Lake Nature Park. The meeting will be held at 7:30 p.m. at the Jewish Community Center at 4330 Cedar Lake Road in St. Louis Park.

FIGURE 8. First map of Cedar Lake Park, 1989. Image courtesy of Jon Finn.

it showed how close SCLP was to attaining its fund-raising goal. Anyone headed across the bridge instantly became aware that a new park was in the making.

That same year, the group created another symbol: the "Save Cedar Lake Park" button. Soon these green-and-white buttons were popping up everywhere. Volunteers carted a bushel full over to the state capitol and cajoled legislators to wear them.

Early in the campaign, the spiral emerged as a potent symbol of the group's energy. It captured the essence of the momentum that quickly grew as the project expanded into the community, draw-

**FIGURE 9.** Save Cedar Lake Park button. Image courtesy of CLPA.

ing people from all walks of life into its vortex. It popped up in literature and on T-shirts. Later, the spiral would be incorporated into the design of the Cedar Lake Park Memorial Grove (see chapter 10).

Volunteer artists designed caps and folksy T-shirts with *Nurture Nature* emblazoned on the back and a mini-park on the front that included foxes and snakes. The fox came to symbolize the possibilities for creating habitat for wildlife in the midst of an urban center.

**FIGURE 10.** CLPA Nurture Nature mini-park label. Image courtesy of CLPA.

# 3

## Buying the Land

HAVING BOUGHT SOME TIME TO ORGANIZE, GATHER INFORMATION, and seek support, Save Cedar Lake Park now needed a fiscal partner. It contacted several sources, asking them to act as agents to hold the land in trust while SCLP continued raising funds.

Early in 1990, The Nature Conservancy (TNC) stepped forward. The SCLP project fit the TNC mission *"to preserve the plants, animals and natural communities that represent the diversity of life on Earth by protecting the lands and waters they need to survive."* Traditionally, TNC focused on buying up pristine land or land with endangered habitat and holding it until a suitable buyer could come forward. As an agent for this venture, TNC stretched its mission statement to include the old railroad yard, even though it wasn't pristine land, nor did it contain any endangered species. For over a year and a half, TNC acted as an umbrella under which the Park Board and SCLP continued to negotiate with the railroad over purchasing the land.

Since MPRB and SCLP were working so closely together, they decided to form an informal partnership (henceforth colloquially known as "The Partnership"). The Park Board provided briefings to SCLP. It informed SCLP about upcoming technical advisory committees and invited the group to send representatives. MPRB also sent staff to SCLP meetings to brief it on any changes to the project. For its part, SCLP kept the Park Board informed about its fundraising activities and any concerns that it had about the direction of the project. The Partnership's goal was to present a united front during negotiations and to work in concord for the future park.

### Managing Negotiations

Officials at Burlington Northern turned negotiations over to a subsidiary: Glacier Park. Meanwhile, the Minneapolis Park Board—in order to strengthen its own position—asked the Metropolitan Council to include the property in its Regional Recreational Open Space System. In November of 1989, the Metropolitan Council voted to add the Cedar Lake Park property to its system. That December, the Park Board designated the property for acquisition. All of these maneuverings meant that the Partnership could claim a right of first refusal to purchase the land. In June of 1991, when Glacier Park officially put the land up for sale, SCLP was able to use these actions to dissuade two potential developers from doing business with Glacier Park. Through this sometimes contentious process, SCLP members struggled to remain positive.

One stumbling block to acquiring the land was the issue of municipal jurisdictions. SCLP's original goal was to acquire twenty-eight acres of land directly north of Cedar Lake in Minneapolis. During negotiations, Glacier Park expanded the deal to include an additional twenty acres of land west of Cedar Lake. Most of that land was in St. Louis Park. The Park Board was understandably concerned about encroaching upon another city's jurisdiction. Eventually the Partnership persuaded the Metropolitan Council to add these twenty acres to its Open Space System and couple them to the Minneapolis section.

### Sustaining the Energy

Such protracted negotiations tested the group's mettle. Often citizen-led initiatives fail because participants become discouraged by the enormity of the task. Fortunately, SCLP found ways to persevere. "People often underestimate their ability to sustain a volunteer project over a long period of time," one of SCLP's chief negotiators reflected. "Too often they start out seeing how big the whole job is rather than how tiny each little piece of it is. If you put enough bits together, ultimately it gets to a point where effective change can happen." SCLP sustained momentum for almost three years. How did they manage it?

SCLP created subcommittees to work on different aspects of the project. While one group worked on land negotiations, another developed fundraising proposals. Still another focused on connecting to the wider metropolitan community. SCLP's subcommittees acted semi-autonomously. Such flexibility and willingness to delegate authority became a hallmark of the organization.

### Creating the *Figure 8*

Creative ideas create energy. One imaginative concept that came out of the group's brainstorming sessions was the *Figure 8*. Pictorially, the Grand Rounds can be viewed as an elongated circle around the city. The proposed Cedar Lake Regional Trail, running from St.

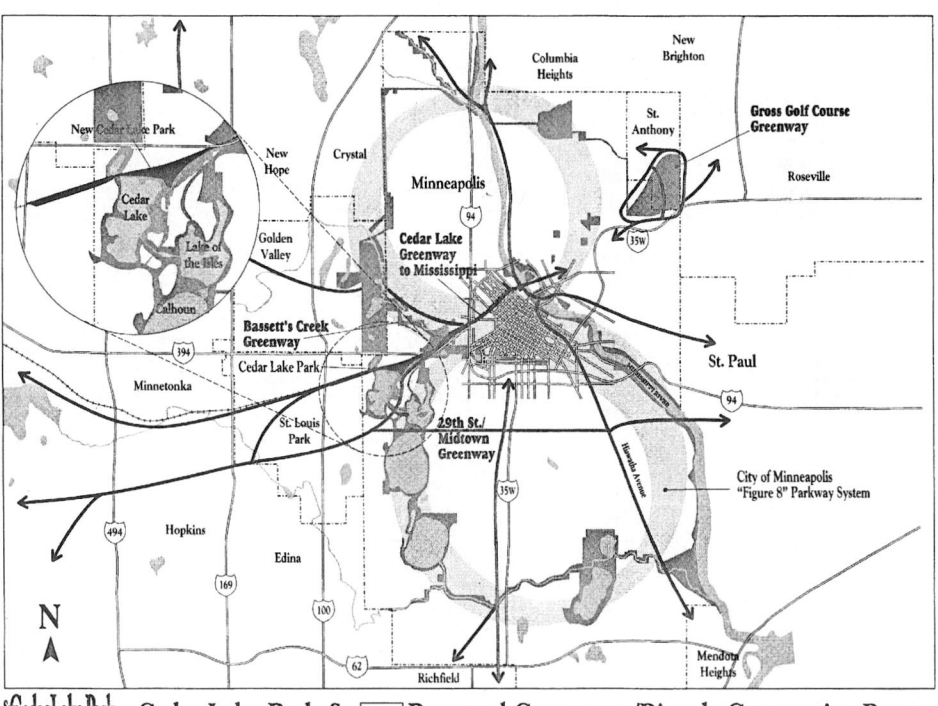

**Cedar Lake Park** Cedar Lake Park & ➡ Proposed Greenways/Bicycle Commuting Routes
377-9522

**FIGURE 11.** *Figure 8* map. Image courtesy of CLPA.

Louis Park to the Mississippi River, would draw a line through the center of the Grand Rounds and turn it into a *Figure 8*.

The idea was simple, yet transformative. Creating a green belt stretching from the western edge of Minneapolis through the center of the city to the Mississippi River would create endless possibilities for commuting and recreational use. Such a band would draw in the surrounding neighborhoods, which would naturally seek to connect to it, thereby establishing a regional network of trails that would bind together the metropolitan area. The *Figure 8* concept became the lynchpin of SCLP's trail campaign strategy.

### Hiring Staff

Over time, coordinating the diverse elements of the campaign took its toll on the core members of the all-volunteer group. (During the drive, one young daughter of a founder called her father a "park addict.") When the workload became too much to handle, SCLP hired a volunteer coordinator to produce the newsletter, coordinate meetings, staff outreach events, and oversee a myriad of activities. This enabled the overworked SCLP core group to focus on planning and fundraising.

### Persuading Large Donors

By 1990, SCLP had acquired a broad donor base. But to make its goal, SCLP needed a few large private contributions. Members began making calls and setting up meetings with select individuals. Prospects looked good. As one member put it, "The rich don't mind being asked to give, but they must be assured that the projects they support have a good chance to succeed."

SCLP had created a clear mission statement, well-structured organization, and large membership base; it had also showed political acumen in forging partnerships with public agencies and tenacity in negotiating with the railroad. These qualities convinced several wealthy citizens, a few of whom asked to remain anonymous, to donate large sums of money to purchase the land. Finally, with almost $500,000 in pledges, SCLP was ready to approach state legislators.

### Acquiring State Funding and Purchasing the Land

Many a group petitions the state with an empty hat, asking government to fill it. Save Cedar Lake Park approached legislators with a hat one-third full. Raising large amounts of private money showed SCLP's strength and commitment. Legislators took note.

During the 1991 session, SCLP members took turns lobbying legislators at the state capitol. Volunteers handed out Save Cedar Lake Park buttons. SCLP members tirelessly lobbied both sides of the aisle in both houses. When the project was on a committee's agenda, SCLP's sixteen-page booklet would be lying on the table in front of them. Dozens of activists, clad in Save Cedar Lake Park T-shirts and wearing green-and-white buttons, would stand in the back of the room, silently urging legislators to support the project.

At twelve seconds to the close of session on May 20, 1991, the Minnesota State Legislature approved a bill with a $1.2 million provision to acquire the forty-eight acres of land north and west of Cedar Lake. In all, Save Cedar Lake Park helped amass $1.7 million in private contributions and state appropriations, paving the way for the Minneapolis Park and Recreation Board to purchase the land. On November 25, 1991, the Minneapolis Park and Recreation Board officially established Cedar Lake Park.

**FIGURE 12.** SCLP presents check to MPRB on November 20, 1991. Image courtesy of Dorothy Childers.

Cedar Lake Park is a gift from the citizens of Minneapolis to the citizens of Minnesota," said Park Superintendent David Fisher after accepting a check for $487,000 from members of Save Cedar Lake Park. Park Commissioner Patti Baker (second from right) also looked on. To fulfill SCLP's $533,000 commitment and move forward with the closing, the James Ford Bell Foundation donated $5,000 and made an interest-free loan for about $46,000. SCLP was able to repay the loan by the end of 1992.

**FIGURE 13.** MPRB, Cedar Lake Park sign.
Image courtesy of CLPA.

# 4
## Creating a Park

SAVE CEDAR LAKE PARK PLANNED TO DISBAND ONCE THE PARK HAD been established. With the land purchased, many felt their work was done. "Long-term projects like this take on the aspect of a train ride," the group's volunteer coordinator remarked. "Some people board the train and ride for a while, then get off when they reach their station, while others get on and take a seat." Many founders saw the establishment of the park as their cue to step away.

But for others, the park had become a touchstone. To realize their dreams, they would need to nurture the land. In the campaign to establish the park, the group had postponed addressing many critical issues; now these came to the fore. Many members were excited to tackle the next stage, and so they continued on.

### Developing Plans for the Park

Having completed the lobbying, fundraising, and negotiations to create the park, SCLP moved to develop the park and connecting trail. In 1989, the Park Board had convened the Cedar Lake Parks & Trails Citizens' Advisory Committee (CAC). That group—in fits and starts—would continue meeting for almost seven years. Work was divided into four phases:

I. Conceptual Trail Design (1992)
II. Philosophy and Design Principles (1992–1993)
III. Park & Trail Planning (1993)
IV. Park & Trail Planning Construction (1994–1996)

Because of the critical need to create construction documents for the trail (federal monies for trail construction had to be spent within a certain time period), park planning had to wait. For the sake of the narrative, the phases dealing with the trail will be covered in chapter 6.

During Phase II, the CAC crafted a philosophical framework for future development of the park. Building on previous work, CAC members focused on articulating the principles that inspired the park's creation.

SCLP and the CAC became deeply entwined. SCLP's Mission Statement and Organizational Guidelines became the foundation for the CAC's working strategy. Although park staff often provided guidance and assistance, Save Cedar Lake Park was the CAC's driving force. With its president acting as the citizen leader of the CAC, and several members obtaining seats, the line between the two groups became blurred.

Starting with the lake itself and working outward from there, the CAC discussed issues such as: water quality, land use, vegetation and wildlife, connection to other green spaces, and how humans (and their pets) entered into the mix. The goal was to preserve, protect, and enhance this unique lake and its surrounding environment. The CAC met monthly for over two years to fashion a framework for the park.

On March 1, 1993, thirty-five members of the CAC signed the Cedar Lake Park & Trails Statement of Philosophy and Design Principles (see Appendix B).

*Key principles*

**PROTECT** and improve the water resources and soils.

**RECONSTITUTE** a variety of native plant communities that reflect lake, wetland, prairie, savanna, woodland, and forest ecosystems.

**MANAGE** the plant and animal communities for their long-term integrity, stability, and beauty.

**CONNECT** ecosystems, green corridors, and trail systems.

MINIMIZE human artifacts and amenities within the conservancy.

INTEGRATE the surrounding land uses to complement the park.

FACILITATE learning experiences in the park.

CELEBRATE people living in harmony with nature and each other.

The momentum created by this work spurred the CAC to tackle its next task. To fulfill the goals of the Statement of Philosophy, the group needed to drill deeper. Just what was the quality of the water and soil? What had happened over the last 150 years (since European settlement) to affect the ecosystems in and around Cedar Lake? What was the best way to effectively manage and protect the plant and animal communities, especially given the porous borders surrounding the park? And how was the area to be connected to the green corridors and parks in surrounding area? Such questions went beyond the expertise of the CAC. It needed professional help.

### Expanding the Partnership

At this crucial juncture, the Minneapolis Department of Public Works (MPW)—which would oversee construction of the trail—joined the Partnership. These three stakeholders (MPRB, MPW, and SCLP) held a competition in the spring of 1993 to select a landscape architect firm to design the park and adjoining trail.

Park and Trail CAC members spent the day reviewing over 40 proposals from local and national landscape architects. During the marathon session, the Partnership sought designs that reflected the philosophy of the project: an urban nature park with a connecting trail at its edge. At the end of the day, they chose five finalists who best understood that essential concept.

On May 3, 1993, the finalists presented their designs before SCLP and CAC members, as well as staff from the Minneapolis Park Board and Public Works. A selection committee—composed of three representatives from MPRB, two from MPW, and two from SCLP—met the next day. It chose Jones & Jones/Richard Haag Associates of Seattle, Washington, to design Cedar Lake Park.

**FIGURE 14.** Reviewing proposals from landscape architects. Image courtesy of CLPA.

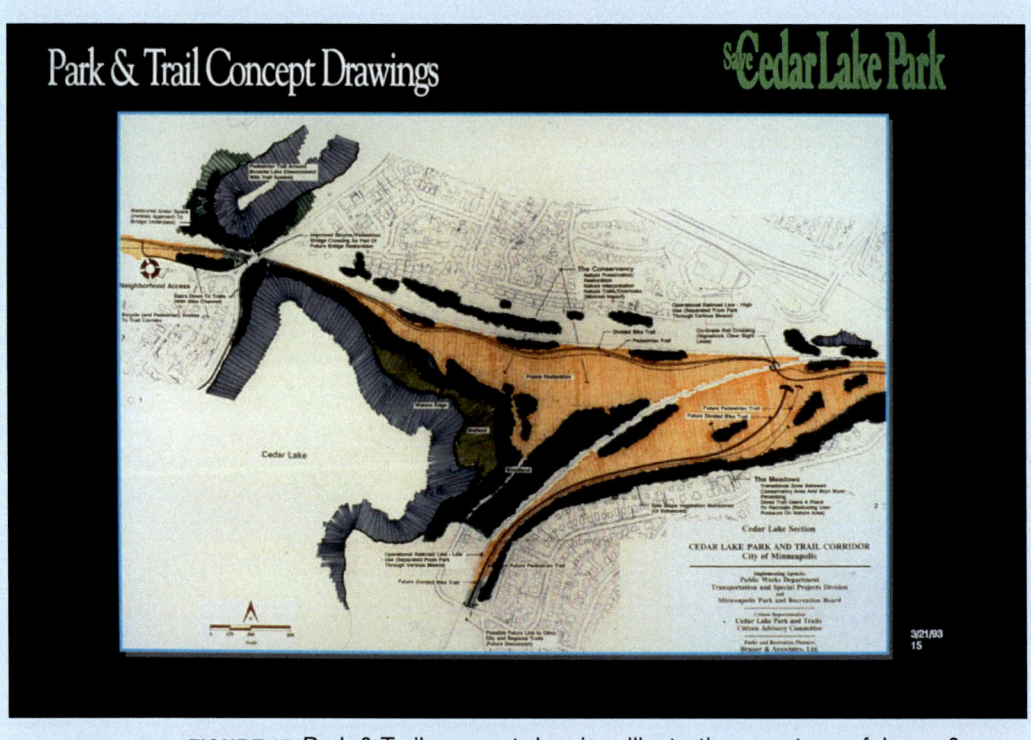

**FIGURE 15.** Park & Trail concept drawing. Illustration courtesy of Jones & Jones/Richard Haag Associates.

A consortium of public staff, private citizens, and professional designers oversaw the planning and construction of the trail system and the contouring and seeding of the park prairie. At the same time, this group labored to realize the potential of the Statement of Philosophy and create a concept master plan that would examine the park's past and present, and guide it into the future.

### Drafting the Concept Master Plan

After two years of instruction and discussion with water and soil experts, as well as landscape architects, the Citizens' Advisory Committee drafted a comprehensive 100-year vision for the Park: the Cedar Lake Park Concept Master Plan. (To view the master plan, see www.cedarlakepark.org.)

Based on the ideas found in the Cedar Lake Park & Trails Statement of Philosophy and Design Principles, the master plan provided a comprehensive guide for developing the park. It examined the history of the area as a transportation corridor. It took an extensive inventory of the land surrounding the lake. It described current land use and effective ways to foster future use. Finally, with sketches and illustrations, it offered recommendations for physically reshaping the park to successfully restore native habitat. The master plan created a blueprint for developing a twenty-first century nature park.

A second generation of citizens has relied on this document to help develop the park. For example, using the language of the master plan on restoration and management, one member was able to obtain state grants for the group to restore the maple-basswood forest on the northeast shoreline. The plan also provided information to aid members in planting native-species wildflowers and grasses in the prairie. This second generation has relied on the master plan to continue the mission.

# 5

# *Keeping the Vision Alive*

WHAT ACCOUNTS FOR THE STAYING POWER OF THE CEDAR LAKE Park organization? Many point to the positive outlook that infused the project with such energy. Setbacks were not failures. "When you've taken a car trip and encountered a detour," one member pointed out, "has it ever prevented you from reaching your destination? A lot of people saw detour signs and read them as dead ends. We didn't."

Save Cedar Lake Park always articulated its ideas positively: it was not against private development—it was for a public park. "The group understood that people get tired of always having to react to things that are being done to them," one discerning member noted. "What was needed was to get way ahead of the curve by asking what could be and should be the vision, and then to articulate that vision." He went on. "When an adversarial approach is taken with people who haven't yet caught the vision, it keeps them in that adversarial position. It doesn't allow them to change. Creating enemies creates a lot of baggage. It weighs organizations down. In the long run, it can pull the project down. By emphasizing the positive, we made the effort more enjoyable." He concluded, "If we hadn't been having fun, we wouldn't have been able to sustain the effort."

### Connecting to Universal Values

A key to SCLP's success was its ability to articulate a clear vision that connected to people's deepest values. SCLP reshaped the mission statement (a review of the archives unearthed at least three itera-

36

tions). While drafting the design principles, they honed the language to a sharp edge. "There was a series of sessions just focusing on design criteria," one leader recalled. "People said it wouldn't happen. That people couldn't get excited about it. That they'd get bored. Far from it—people loved being a part of it. That was the most exciting part. We spent a whole evening talking about how to phrase a sentence so that we could say exactly what we wanted to say."

"I think one of the keys to the organization's staying power was that the leaders of the group were not on some kind of personal ego trip," one founder mused. "We understood that our most valuable work as leaders was to create a structure through which other people could make contributions and shine. The key leaders were very good at sublimating their egos and allowing others the time and space to express themselves and reach a robust consensus."

The time invested in creating the mission statement and organizational guidelines proved invaluable. With clearly stated objectives, the 52-member Citizens' Advisory Committee reached almost every decision by consensus. The process meant that all voices would be heard. Achieving consensus was bedrocked on staying faithful to the mission—asking how the particular issue related to a deeper value or how it clarified the vision.

In the winter of 1992, the Park Board sponsored a workshop that focused on the natural, historical, and social forces that could impact the new nature park. MPRB's Jeff Lee gave an overview of Cedar Lake's water quality and voiced his concern about algae blooms in the lake due to urban runoff and drainage from Twin Lake to the west. Park Environmentalist Al Singer's bore samplings confirmed that most of the park's soil was railroad fill, along with underlying sand and gravel. Only certain kinds of native prairie plants would survive in such an environment. An expert from a suburban nature preserve warned of the damage that can occur due to dumping of unwanted pets and unchecked growth of certain animal species. Rail expert Phil Qualy spoke about the history of the Minneapolis & St. Louis' Cedar Lake Yards and the impact it left in the area. Finally, Ron Bowen from Prairie Restorations, Inc., explained how to best establish and maintain a prairie/savannah with such soil conditions. In other forums, landscape architects such as Diana Balmori and Richard Haag explored ways in which landscape forms can enhance people's spiritual connection with the land.

## Staying Ahead of the Curve

Many in SCLP recall the years between 1992 and 1996 as a constant whirl of meetings. As the park and trail construction deadlines neared, the group struggled to keep up with the pace. Besides the monthly CAC meeting and SCLP steering committee meetings (most of the core group were also part of the CAC), SCLP also held a planning meeting every Friday morning at 7:00. Just making that morning meeting was an arduous task for some, but the group knew that to make an impact, it needed to be prepared.

While SCLP's membership list grew to over two thousand names, its core group was never more than a dozen or so. Events and workshops often brought in large crowds, but SCLP's steering committee meetings seldom drew more than ten attendees. While this may seem like a small number, it is not an unusual for citizen groups. Burnout is always a concern and volunteer organizations must be on the lookout for new blood. When some get off the train, others need to come on board.

One of the group's strengths was its internal structure. Although the Articles of Incorporation list the board of directors as the legal authority for the group's actions, in reality, the board's role was minimal. It met only once or twice a year, mainly to elect officers and authorize funds to pay for initiatives approved by the steering committee. Real power rested in the steering committee. It would analyze issues, make decisions, and propose actions. While the board was restricted in size, the steering committee was open to anyone who came through the door. To handle such flux, it's essential to have a clear mission statement and detailed set of organizational guidelines.

The steering committee usually met before an upcoming CAC session to discuss the agenda, plan strategy, and play out possible

**FIGURE 16.** Bluebird in the Cedar Lake Park Prairie. Image courtesy of CLPA.

For years the Minneapolis Chapter of the Audubon Society dreamed of purchasing land for a bird sanctuary in the city. When its members heard about the effort to save Cedar Lake Park, they voted to donate their entire sanctuary fund of $15,000 toward its purchase. Audubon members continue to maintain an active presence in the park, leading bird-watching tours and taking bird counts. As part of a drive to reintroduce Eastern bluebirds, they erect bluebird houses every spring, take nesting counts, and document bluebird migratory patterns. Every fall, they dismantle the boxes and refurbish them for the next year. As part of their educational mission, Audubon members often contribute articles to the *CLPA Update*.

scenarios. Often Park Board or city staff would brief the steering committee on changes in policy. With that information, the group worked to develop strategies to counter possible fallout. During all this, SCLP's core group always kept in mind that it represented thousands of people whose contributions kept the organization functioning.

### Dealing with Disappointments

SCLP took on several other projects during this time. Not all were successful. Not long after the creation of Cedar Lake Park, the Bliss property came up for sale. This land, with its own interesting history, abutted Cedar Lake Park just west of Ewing Avenue. Since the property was contiguous, many thought it would make a fine addition to the park. SCLP scheduled time at meetings to map out strategy. It employed the tactics that had proved so successful in saving Cedar Lake Park. First the group named and claimed the land as the "Ewing Wetlands." Next it sought to build support among the surrounding neighbors. It even created a fundraising mechanism. Ultimately, these measures came to naught and the land was sold to a developer who built condos on it.

A second piece of property came up for sale shortly after on the east side of Cedar Lake. This was known as "the blue house." At one time it was owned by the Minneapolis & St. Louis Railway and housed the Cedar Lake Yards' superintendent. While SCLP saw this as another wonderful addition to Greater Cedar Lake Park (part of this property actually juts out into the Kenilworth Corridor), it too was eventually sold for private use.

The group faced another challenge when the Cedar Lake Regional Trail was constructed. Preliminary plans showed the western terminus of the trail rising up out of the rail corridor and connecting to a pedestrian bridge in St. Louis Park. A couple of homeowners objected to a trailhead so close to their property. SCLP attended meetings at the St. Louis Park City Hall to plead its case, but the homeowners prevailed. MPRB planner Gary Criter was forced to scrap plans at the eleventh hour and scramble to come up with an alternate trailhead. He quickly drew a plan that connected the trail to the Highway 100 service road. (Ten years later, St. Louis Park completed a ramp from the very same pedestrian bridge down to the trail.) The lesson learned? It only takes a few people to effect change—or stall a project.

### Celebrating Success

SCLP successes far outweighed its failures and its leaders stressed the need to celebrate achievements. One such celebration occurred on July 26, 1992, when SCLP and the Park Board co-sponsored the Cedar Lake Park Land Acquisition Celebration. For many months, a committee worked on logistics for the party: for example, securing a venue, obtaining a stage, and contacting speakers.

During this planning, a concern arose. Aware of their fiscal obligations to donors, some questioned the propriety of spending SCLP funds on a party. One member, new to the group, argued that it should be possible to manage the project and not spend donor funds. As he rattled on, stating his case, he noticed smiles appearing. He realized he'd talked himself into leading the project.

Others stepped forward to help. One member pledged to obtain needed supplies—hot dogs, chips, condiments—gratis or at a reduced rate. "I'm not afraid to beg for a good cause," she quipped. As a result of her efforts, all of the supplies and most of the food were donated.

To help celebrate the creation of the park, the Minnesota Volkssports Association sponsored a Walk & Roll for Cedar Lake Park. The pre-celebration event attracted 295 Volksmarchers who hiked or biked to the site. The event raised about $1,000 for SCLP. Around noon, they marched in with their flags flying to add to the festivities.

Everything worked out perfectly; even the weather cooperated. During the event, SCLP's president read a letter to the crowd sent by Governor Arne Carlson. In it he wrote, "You should take great pride

**FIGURE 17.** Volksmarchers Walk & Roll patch. Image courtesy of CLPA.

**FIGURE 18.** Governor Arne Carlson embracing Save Cedar Lake Park members. Image courtesy of CLPA.

in an accomplishment that demonstrates all the best about citizen involvement and public/private cooperation." On the platform, speakers praised SCLP's role in acquiring the land. Meanwhile, folks ambled from the stage to the food tent to grab some food and chat. Children with painted faces played beneath the stage, oblivious to the speeches above. On that day, the gathered throng basked in the afterglow of what they had achieved.

Such celebrations renewed enthusiasm and helped bind the group together. Many who came to the celebrations and annual meetings did not actively participate, but they demonstrated their love for the park just by showing up. Buoyed by the infectious enthusiasm, they took the message to their friends and neighbors. This loose-knit network provided vital financial support to maintain the organization. "It's far easier to build something than it is to maintain it," one member observed. "Everyone wants their money to go for bricks and mortar. No one wants to pay for upkeep." The support these members provided helped sustain the effort.

### Volunteering Stories

While engaged in the effort, many people came to realize the role they could play in enhancing the city. "I think the most important legacy is the spirit that supersedes the place," one member observed. "If we can pass on the spirit, the education, the challenge, then this place is just the start of something big. We see the project as a kind of parent plant that sends out these rhizomes. Rise up and rhizome—not just here but around the world!"

Some found their calling in nurturing the land. "I'd never volunteered for anything before," one member admitted, "but once I started working on Cedar Lake Park, I found the land nurtured *me*. So often, we identify ourselves by the work we do. When people ask me, 'What do you do for a living?' I answer, 'I'm a Cedar Lake Park volunteer.' I found my bliss caring for the park."

Some efforts had serendipitous consequences for those involved. After the Partnership selected the landscape architectural firm of Jones & Jones to oversee the park and trail design, the project manager—who had roots in Minneapolis—flew in and spent several weeks in Minnesota. After the project was complete, he relocated to Minneapolis and became a member of SCLP. With his expertise and background, he often worked behind the scenes providing insight into design issues and creating sketches (see *figure 40*) to jumpstart projects. Although he eventually moved back to the West Coast, he has kept in contact and continues to be a valuable resource.

Some just couldn't stay away. One member left the board because the demands on his time were just too great. Yet the vision refused to leave him. Soon, he was back attending steering committee meetings and planning sessions. He oversaw the publication of the master plan and served a stint as the group's president. Eventually he moved to another part of the country, where he became executive director of a community group dedicated to preserving a wild and remote corner of that state. He too has kept in touch and continues to provide guidance.

Some moved right in and got to work. As one volunteer recalled, "My husband and I moved into the Bryn Mawr neighborhood in 1989 and had lived there only two weeks. I had been talking to my next-door neighbor, saying how wonderful it was for the City of Minneapolis to have saved this open space behind our neighborhood. She said, 'The city doesn't own this. The railroad owns it and they're trying to sell it.' And I said, 'Oh my God! We have to do something about this.' She told me there was a group starting up and that I should talk to one of my neighbors down the street. I left my yard, walked right up to her house, knocked on her door and introduced myself and said, 'We've got to do something about this property back here.' She said, 'Come in. Have I got a deal for you!' Two hours later, I walked out as the volunteer membership chair."

Sometimes a sign brings them in. One day in 1991, while driving over the ancient Cedar Lake Parkway Bridge, a new arrival in Bryn Mawr caught sight of the large thermometer looming over Ewing

Avenue that showed how much money was needed to create Cedar Lake Park. He made out a swath of red paint that seemed to be inching toward its goal. Later, before a performance at the Guthrie Theatre, he was chatting with a woman next to him. Mentioning the sign, he told her how exciting it must be to create a new park. The woman's eyes lit up. She just happened to be the volunteer chair! Never at a loss, she dug out some membership forms and invited him to the group's next meeting. "The first meeting I went to was the annual meeting in January of 1992," he recalled. "I saw a great slide show about the park and then I heard how the Cedar Lake Regional Trail would turn the Grand Rounds into a *Figure 8*. As an avid bicyclist, I was hooked."

Another SCLP member later got into local politics. As a park commissioner, he sought to refocus the priorities of the city's transportation system. He advocated transforming the city's transportation paradigm. Instead of cars, he proposed placing pedestrians and bicyclists on the top of the pyramid. He sought to increase funding for nonmotorized transit. "Let's get people out of their cars," he said. Later, he served on the Kenilworth Trail Citizens' Advisory Committee, where he predicted, "The Kenilworth will be the most heavily used trail in the city." He helped found the coalition that oversaw the development of the Midtown Greenway, a trail that has sparked economic development in South Minneapolis. One beautiful summer day, while he was out bicycling with his red-haired son, he ran into a fellow bicyclist out in the park. "I just can't help but smile," he said. "Look at all the happy people out here. It really makes it worth it."

No doubt the group had a bit of luck in recruiting its pool of talent, but people excited by a vision seem to serendipitously come together to effect change. As Margaret Meade so famously said, "A small group of thoughtful people could change the world. Indeed, it's the only thing that ever has."

**Renaming and Refocusing the Group**

Creating the nature park had been Save Cedar Lake Park's original goal. But after the park was created, the situation remained very fluid. SCLP decided not to disband as it had planned. After overseeing the design of the trail system to ensure that it would enhance the park and not gobble it up, SCLP felt it needed to develop long-delayed initiatives, such as creating a Big Woods Maple-Basswood forest on the northeastern edge of the lake and reintroducing native-species plants in the Cedar Lake Park prairie. Faced with these obligations, the membership voted in 1994 to become a permanent citizens' advocacy organization with a new name: the Cedar Lake Park Association (CLPA).

**FIGURE 19.** New masthead of *Cedar Lake Park Update.* Image courtesy of CLPA.

# Cedar Lake Park

**UPDATE**

**Winter 1997/98**                                                                                      **Volume 10, No. 1**

*Small masthead change reflects larger conceptual shift:*

# From saving the park, to building our vision

BY JIM McPHERSON

As you can see, the word, "Save," that has headed the Cedar Lake Park Update since its inception, has been deleted. "Save Cedar Lake Park" was also the first name of the Cedar Lake Park Association of 65 citizens who gathered to save the old railroad yards near Cedar Lake as parklands. Thanks to an outpouring of community support during the early '90s, both financial and volunteer, they were able to save the land from development.

Now that the park has been saved, the focus is on restoration and education. It was over a hundred years ago, in 1883, when Minneapolis citizens first convinced the State Legislature to form the Minneapolis Board of Park Commissioners who conceived the city's first 100-year plan for preserving parklands. The Cedar Lake Park Association has since developed a 100-year Concept Master Plan for restoring and building the park.

This plan reflects thousands of hours of volunteer time — more than 2,600 this year alone — and the Cedar Lake Park Association is committed to working with the Minneapolis Park and Recreation Board (MPRB) to increase volunteerism in this year

Cedar Lake Park is a unique model for citizen participation in the planning and development of a special place to relax, reflect and nurture nature.

ahead. We are also working to raise funds and consciousness to realize the CLPA's stated vision: "...to restore the lands and waters and create a new community with nature, through which we can transform ourselves, our city and our society."

As we look ahead to the next century and millennium, we can only begin to imagine what lies ahead. However, we have begun to plan for exciting times of transition with more and more diverse people using the park. Our goal is to bring people and nature together in a harmonious community.

Further, our communications are evolving, with new editorship for this newsletter. We would like to thank Laurie Lundy a great deal for her energy, enthusiasm and countless hours as editor. Her work writing and editing articles and coordinating with the printers and the volunteers, who sort and mail out the newsletter, has helped our Association communicate our ideas and objectives. We thank her for her tremendous contribution to Save Cedar Lake Park.

*Watch for your invitation with the time and place!*

## Annual Meeting set for January 28

We look forward to seeing you!

**Federal Highway Administration**

**Environmental Excellence Award 1995**

For Excellence in Bicycle/Pedestrian Programs:

Cedar Lake Trail

**Cedar Lake Park Association**
**Minneapolis Park and Recreation Board**
**City of Minneapolis**
**Hennepin County Regional Rail Authority**
**Metropolitan Park and Open Space Commission**
**Minnesota Department of Transportation**

This trail is a 5.6-kilometer (3.5-mile) off-road commuter route from the suburb of St. Louis Park to downtown Minneapolis. The trail provides two one-way bicycle and skater paths, and a separate pathway for joggers and pedestrians. A local citizens' organization, the Cedar Lake Park Association, raised a third of the purchase price for the corridor, and the Minnesota Department of Transportation is providing the remainder. This rail-to-trail conversion is a model of local community action which resulted in environmental and transportation benefits to a metropolitan area.

Federal Highway Administrator

April 21, 1995

**FIGURE 20.** Federal Highway Administration Trail Award. Image courtesy of CLPA.

# 6
## The Trail

REALIZING IT NEEDED TO GARNER BROAD PUBLIC SUPPORT FOR ITS embryonic nature park, the Cedar Lake Park Association* decided early on to link the park to other green spaces through a system of trails or "linear parks." Although CLPA wanted to focus on the park, the group realized it had to put park development aside to work on the trail. However, as a part of trail construction, the park would be contoured and seeded—so the two projects were really interwoven.

Almost as soon as the ink was dry on the land purchase agreement, the Cedar Lake Park Association resolved to raise private funds to create what would become the first federally funded non-motorized commuter trail in the nation. Starting at Highway 100 in St. Louis Park (see *figure 1*), the trail would run east alongside the Burlington Northern mainline tracks and continue through downtown Minneapolis to its terminus at the Mississippi River. The trail would bring people from the city and the suburbs to Cedar Lake Park. It would promote bicycle commuting to downtown and to the University of Minnesota, as well as spur the creation of connecting trails. Linking the lakes to the river would be a boon to recreational bicyclists and pedestrians. Because of its significance for expanding nonmotorized transportation throughout the metropolitan area, CLPA pushed to name it the Cedar Lake *Regional* Trail.

In 1992, the Partnership approached the state legislature for a $700,000 grant. The state grant was contingent on securing federal

*For the sake of consistency, the term "Cedar Lake Park Association" will be used from now on, even though some of the events in this chapter took place before the name change.

funding as well as matching private contributions. CLPA agreed to raise the private match. New federal funds had become available through the 1991 Intermodal Surface Transportation Efficiency Act (ISTEA). The act was designed to redirect federal resources to non-motorized commuter transportation. Other groups applied for and received federal funds for trail construction before the Partnership did, but all of them had to turn the funds back because they could not meet the requirements or timeline. The MPRB/MPW/CLPA Partnership became the first in the nation to actually use the funds to construct a commuter trail.

To raise funds, CLPA once again appealed to its base. One member who raised funds for the trail recalled, "I'd go to possible donors and throw out a high figure to them, then wait to see what they would respond with. So it wasn't would you donate, but how *much* would you donate." This strategy elicited large contributions (such as those pledged by the Hedberg Family Foundation) and went a long way toward funding the trail.

But funding was not the only issue. CLPA often found itself addressing the concerns of businesses along the proposed corridor. Luckily it had built strong connections to the business community as well as contacts with Burlington Northern. The railroad had legitimate liability concerns: for much of its length, the trail would run adjacent to BN's track. CLPA members met several times with the railroad executives to listen to their concerns and propose solutions.

Again, the group needed to lobby state legislators. Any time the trail was on the agenda, the coordinator would have volunteers to don their old Save Cedar Lake Park T-shirts and stand in the back of the committee room as silent advocates. CLPA worked hard to persuade wary outstate lawmakers that the trail would be a boon not just for the city, but for outlying communities as well.

Ultimately, the Partnership was able to leverage $500,000 of private funds from over 1,300 CLPA members to match state and federal funding. In total, CLPA helped raise over $1.6 million of public and private money to build the trail.

### Designing the Trail

In 1993, the Partnership had selected Jones & Jones/Richard Haag Associates to design the park and trail. Jones & Jones would be required to create a concept master plan for the park, while simultaneously developing construction documents for the trail—all within seven months. That schedule proved daunting.

In the summer of 1993, the project manager for Jones & Jones began to scout the park. His charge was to build a trail at the edge of the prairie alongside a rail corridor into an urban center. He had to create an integrated trail alignment that would enhance the character of the new park, while conforming to the requirements of federal, state, and local government agencies.

He designed three undulating, serpentine ribbons tracing along the edge of Cedar Lake Park. The separated paths—two ten-foot lanes for bicyclists and one nine-foot lane for pedestrians—set a

**FIGURE 21.** Jones & Jones project manager working in the park. Image courtesy of Dorothy Childers.

**FIGURE 22.** Groundbreaking for the Cedar Lake Regional Trail. Image courtesy of Dorothy Childers.

standard for future trails. He integrated the trail into the park by sculpting the old abandoned railyard into a series of small ridges and swales, thereby crafting a landscape that would foster a rich diversity of plant life. The winding nature of the paths, along with the prairie's varied topography, meant that the trail would be an unobtrusive part of the park's overall design. Space constraints, such as those under the Cedar Lake Parkway Bridge, sometimes required straightening out the trail and narrowing it to one lane for short distances. But overall, this award-winning design addressed the tension between the park lovers and trail enthusiasts by creating a superb trail system through a serene green space.

As with many multiyear, multimillion dollar projects involving numerous agencies and jurisdictions, a few heart-stopping moments did occur. But each time, the Partnership and the landscape architects labored to find common ground to move forward. Initial timelines were stretched. Twice, CLPA members flew to Seattle to meet with Jones & Jones to facilitate deadlines. To speed up the trail design process, work on the Cedar Lake Park Concept Master Plan was shelved. (Members of SCLP would eventually finish the master plan in 1997.) In 1994, Minneapolis Public Works assumed control of the construction phase of the trail. Using Jones & Jones' designs, it completed the project.

On February 17, 1995, the Partnership celebrated the ground-breaking of the trail. That summer, as the *CLPA Update* reported, "Bulldozers in the Park" plowed through the rail yard, obliterating the makeshift prairie and creating a landscape that, for a brief moment, resembled the dark side of the moon (see *figure 23*). The three asphalt trails snaked through the barren earth. Many wondered what had happened to their vision.

Within a few weeks a cover crop of Canada rye broke through the surface. By September, the black-earthed moonscape was a distant

**FIGURE 23.** Bulldozers in the park. Image courtesy of CLPA.

**FIGURE 24.** Looking east from the footbridge in St. Louis Park. Image courtesy of Meredith Montgomery.

memory as the budding prairie began to enshroud the paths (see *figure 24*). The park was reborn.

The new trail stretched from Highway 100 in St. Louis Park to its temporary eastern trailhead on the edge of downtown near Royalston Avenue. (Since there was a bar at the top of the spur, some called it the Lee's Liquor Trailhead.) Plans for the next phase that would link the trail to the West River Parkway were as yet unresolved. (Completing that phase took another sixteen years—see chapter 8.) For now, it was enough to have the trail in place.

### Celebrating the Trail

On September 9, 1995, Mayor Don Fraser led a gaily clad cavalcade through a rainbow-shaped portal of balloons. Bikers, trikers, hikers, and skaters careened down the freshly paved path, winding their way along the serpentine trail before alighting at the base of the speaker's platform at the eastern trailhead. There, in the shadows of downtown skyscrapers, while children played and grown-ups beamed, speaker after speaker lauded the newest addition to the Minneapolis trail system, the Cedar Lake Regional Trail.

The journey to that speaker's platform took much longer than anyone anticipated. The complex task of designing and building the trail involved the Federal Highway Administration, Minnesota Department of Transportation, Hennepin County Regional Railroad Authority, Minneapolis Department of Public Works, Minneapolis Park & Recreation Board, landscape architects, the citizens'

**FIGURE 25.** Opening of the Cedar Lake Trail. Image courtesy of Dorothy Childers.

advisory committee, and the Cedar Lake Park Association. Every change in design meant going through numerous sign-offs. Innovation butted against regulation. Creative solutions created more challenges. Through it all, CLPA played a crucial role in keeping the project moving forward. Although the trail took a year longer than anticipated, it became the first trail to be successfully completed under the new Federal ISTEA program.

Hundreds of people turned out that fall day to celebrate the construction of the Cedar Lake Regional Trail. On the speaker's platform, many singled out CLPA's role in developing the trail, calling it a blueprint for the way public agencies and citizens' groups could work together to get projects done. All of the challenges the Partnership had faced had been overcome and now an off-road, non-motorized bicycle and pedestrian trail was completed from Highway 100 in St. Louis Park to the edge of downtown Minneapolis—pointing like an arrow to the Mississippi River.

---

Several days later, still flush with the excitement of the festivities, one of the founders walked the park's newly dedicated trail. "It was one of the greatest days of my life," he remarked. "I was just blown away that every second or third person I saw was smiling. I thought, 'You know, we have done something wonderful here.' There really is a contrast between how nasty people are on the roads and how wonderful and pleasant they are on the bike trails. People are pretty frustrated with the grimness of the world, and they need the relief these parks can bring. They need the potential for growth and happiness that the parks can provide."

**FIGURE 26.** Looking west from the Kenwood Parkway trailhead. Image courtesy of Meredith Montgomery.

**FIGURE 27.** *Great Northern Railroad tracks on north edge of Cedar Lake going west.* Circa 1900. DETAIL. William Wallof, Hennepin County Library, James K. Hosmer Special Collections Library, Minneapolis Collection, Wallof Collection, W081.

# 7

## The Bridge

By 1999, THE OLD CEDAR LAKE PARKWAY BRIDGE WAS IN SORRY shape. Constructed in 1916, the sturdy bridge had served the Bryn Mawr neighborhood for over eighty-three years. The history of that span—and the road it carried—was almost as old as the city itself.

### The First Bridge

Up until the end of the nineteenth century, a glacial moraine formed a land barrier between Cedar and Brownie Lakes. Cedar Lake Road, the first passageway to the west out of downtown Minneapolis, ran along the top of this ridge en route to Lake Minnetonka (see *figure 4*). To improve rail service out to his luxury hotels on the shores of that lake, James J. Hill ordered work crews to demolish the ridge between Brownie and Cedar Lakes in 1883 and to lay tracks to the west.[15] To span the new gap, they built a wooden bridge (see *figure 27*).[16]

### The Second Bridge

In 1916, to satisfy the demands of local residents, the railroad constructed a sturdier, pony-truss bridge. The Great Northern's original plan called for an unadorned structure, but Minneapolis Park Superintendent Theodore Wirth insisted on a more decorative design and funded the difference in construction costs.[17] That second bridge lasted a long time, but by the late 1990s its cement facing was crumbling. Stop-gap measures attempted to shore up the underside, but chunks of concrete continued to fall off, endangering users of the new Cedar Lake Regional Trail. The old bridge had to go.

**FIGURE 28.** The Second Cedar Lake Parkway Bridge, 1916–2005. Image courtesy of CLPA.

**FIGURE 29.** The Third Cedar Lake Parkway Bridge, November 4, 2004. Image courtesy of Don Beimborn.

### The Third Bridge

In 1999, the city of Minneapolis announced it would replace the bridge. It convened a Cedar Lake Parkway Bridge Citizens' Advisory Committee (known as the Bridge CAC) to help design the new structure and its approaches. CLPA took a prominent part in the committee's work. Based on its work on earlier citizens' advisory committees, CLPA scheduled time on its agenda to receive briefings and formulate strategy and tactics. Thus prepared, representatives could return to the CAC and present coherent concepts that were often adopted.

The Bridge CAC grappled with practical and aesthetic issues. They wanted a bridge that would enhance the character of the area, while discharging its primary duty to safely transport thousands of cars, bicycles, and pedestrians each day.

The crossing was vital. As the only north-south throughway between Dunwoody Avenue to the east and Highway 100 to the west, it served not only the Bryn Mawr neighborhood, but the entire western metro area. The bridge carried the Grand Rounds National Scenic Byway, including both its road and bicycle trail. South of the bridge the road split to become Ewing Avenue and Cedar Lake Parkway. North of the bridge it connected to Theodore Wirth Parkway. Under the bridge ran the BN railroad, the Cedar Lake Regional Trail, and a water channel from Brownie Lake to Cedar Lake. It was a busy place.

---

The Bridge CAC weighed in on the functional design principles for the new bridge. Time and again, it tackled the issue of safety. The old bridge's high arch was difficult to navigate in the winter; cars slipped and slid as they struggled up the grade. The CAC proposed flattening the arch of the new bridge. At the southern approach, two streets—Ewing Avenue and the Cedar Lake Parkway—funneled into it. The old road alignment forced the parkway to a T just before the bridge. The CAC advocated giving precedence to traffic flowing along the parkway and leveling the Ewing Avenue approach.

The Bridge CAC was sensitive to the concerns of nonmotorists.

The Grand Rounds National Scenic Byway bicycle trail intersected the old bridge where the parkway ran into Ewing Avenue. Traffic flow and sightline issues made the crossing one of the most treacherous in the city for bicyclists and pedestrians. The CAC wanted to give bicyclists the option of riding a spur down to the Cedar Lake Regional Trail, going under the bridge, and riding back up to the parkway without encountering motorized traffic.

Local residents expressed concern about access for emergency vehicles during construction. Originally the city was going to close the crossing for a year. Responding to the Bridge CAC's concerns, city staff devised a plan to keep the bridge open during construction.

Then there was the bridge's aesthetics. The old art deco bridge had simple ornamentation with modest pilasters and circular friezes. Many felt the new bridge should incorporate the old artistic embellishments. To give a sense of continuity, planners agreed to recreate the circular friezes on the new bridge. The Bridge CAC proposed creating an area under the bridge that would be functional and provide artistic and educational elements. These ideas were incorporated into the design.

The new design dramatically improved bicycle and pedestrian traffic flow. Two trail spurs connect the south end of the bridge to the Cedar Lake Regional Trail below, creating a bypass that allows bicyclists and pedestrians to move from the trail to the Grand Rounds without encountering an at-grade street crossing. The flattened arch of the bridge and the realignment of Ewing Avenue and Cedar Lake Parkway also make crossing the street safer for those who still want to use the at-grade intersection.

The new bridge proved a vast improvement—above and below. The bridge itself enhanced traffic flow and created better sightlines. Meanwhile, the increase in space underneath the bridge spawned a gathering spot and children's playground. As part of the understructure, engineers constructed a slanting bulwark studded with samples of rock native to Minnesota. Children instantly took to this impromptu rock climb. Above the bulwark, the designers created an educational element.

CLPA helped enhance the Cedar Lake Parkway Bridge as a transportation corridor as well as provide an enjoyable recreational and educational experience under the bridge. While CLPA didn't get all they wanted (the association had advocated making Cedar Lake Parkway a one-way road) it played a valuable role in designing Cedar Lake's third bridge.

### Under the Bridge: Words in Stone

Replacing the old bridge led to an interesting project for CLPA. The Minnesota State Historic Preservation Office (SHPO) had designated the 1916 bridge a historic structure. Although everyone agreed the old bridge needed replacing, SHPO's designation meant that some kind of mitigation would be required. In response, the designers proposed placing a brief history of Cedar Lake on the abutment under the bridge (see *figure 30*). Using a unique molding process,

**FIGURE 30.** Area history, cast in concrete. Image courtesy of Meredith Montgomery.

the text would be cast into the bridge's southern abutments: words etched in stone—or in this case, pressed into concrete.

The designers asked CLPA to provide the historical text and layout. CLPA had just the people to work on the project. One member had been researching the history of the Cedar Lake area for a number of years. Noted history buff Bob Glancy recommended that the researcher contact the Special Collections section of the Minneapolis Public Library (now Hennepin County Library). There he located photographs of long-vanished landmarks like the Cedar Lake Ice House and the Kenwood Hotel, as well as the first bridge to span the gap between Brownie Lake and Cedar Lake. He pulled together material on the area around the bridge and submitted it to SHPO for review. SHPO approved the text with a few minor suggestions.

Another member had experience with laying out text and fonts. The challenge he faced was that the text needed to be visible to the trail users passing under the bridge. The font size would dictate how much of the story could be told. He made a number of suggestions that significantly increased the amount of text that could be presented.

This small group met several times to experiment with font sizes and text alignment. Ultimately they designed twelve panels that briefly described the history of the area. Four panels were displayed in the fall of 2004 when the first section of the new bridge was finished (see *figure 30*). The whole story was unveiled when the new bridge was completed in 2005. Again, CLPA did not get all it wanted: it had advocated adding illustrations to go with the text, but that proved too costly. Still, the panels under the bridge educate trail users in learning about the physical and economic forces that shaped the area.

**FIGURES 31 AND 32.** The Cedar Lake Parkway Bridge, before and after. Images courtesy of Dorothy Childers.

On a brisk winter's day in 2002, CLPA members posed on top of the second Cedar Lake Parkway bridge before it was demolished. Work on the new bridge began in 2003. Keeping the bridge open during construction slowed the pace of the project and the new bridge was not completed until 2005. That spring, CLPA members gathered under the third bridge to document a new milestone in the history of Cedar Lake.

# 8
# *To the River*

**On a Dark and Gloomy Winters' Eve**

In February of 2000, in the dead of winter, a planner from the Minneapolis Department of Public Works came to a meeting of the CLPA steering committee to outline the final phase in constructing the Cedar Lake Regional Trail. The first two phases had been completed in 1995, creating a commuter trail from Highway 100 in St. Louis Park to the western edge of downtown Minneapolis. Planning documents designated the final section as Phase 3, but it became better known as the "to the river" phase. This phase of the trail project would run though a dense downtown infrastructure of private lots, power lines, and brick abutments before reaching its terminus at the West River Parkway above the Mississippi River. It would be a challenge. The news that the MPW planner relayed that night caused quite a stir.

Plans had changed. The original 1989 Wirth Study showed the trail running adjacent to the Burlington Northern corridor until it reached West River Parkway. But Public Works had hit several roadblocks in acquiring land and right-of-ways in the downtown corridor. Because of these impediments, it proposed bringing the trail up out of the corridor at Washington Avenue—three blocks short of the river—and running it along Fourth Avenue until it hit the parkway. The street would be signed and striped for bicycle traffic.

The group sat stunned. This new alignment meant bicyclists would be forced to travel on a city street and negotiate three at-grade crossings before reaching the safety of the West River Parkway Trail.

When group members voiced these concerns, the response was that the road was little used and the striping would suffice to warn cars and trucks that bicycles might be present. As a final note, the planner indicated that the federal funding in place for trail construction was approved for the alignment that MPW proposed. Putting forward an "alternate" alignment could endanger these funds. There appeared to be no recourse.

### Turning Frustration into Action

The steering committee reeled from the impact of the city's proposal. For several months, other concerns took up its energy. Although it discussed the situation from time to time, the group was stymied. Finally, during a committee meeting one Monday evening, the pent-up frustration began spilling out. One member reminded the group that the Hedberg Family Foundation's donation to the trail construction was contingent upon completing the trail to the river *within the corridor*; the Public Works plan was at odds with the donor's stipulation. The group agreed to devote its energy to bringing the trail alignment back into the corridor as originally envisioned. It began sketching out a plan of action. Although it took nearly a year to do so, the CLPA finally began to marshal its forces.

Early in 2001, CLPA approached then Minneapolis Park Commissioner Vivian Mason. CLPA's historical partnership with the Park Board made this an obvious place to begin. However, MPRB had undergone significant changes in staff and policy and was focused on facilities construction and riverfront development. While Commissioner Mason was supportive, she could provide little substantive aid.

In March of 2001, CLPA asked for a meeting with Minneapolis City Council Member Lisa Goodman. Most of the trail lay within the boundaries of her ward. Since the city council held MPW's purse strings, CLPA would need the council's support and Council Member Goodman was an influential member.

At the same time, events were taking place in the park. Unbeknownst to CLPA, one of its members had erected signs in the park

**FIGURE 33.** Trail to the river sign. Image courtesy of CLPA.

warning people that the city's plan to route the trail out of the corridor would bring thousands of commuter and leisure bicyclists, *many of them children*, into the path of dangerous downtown traffic. The signs provoked a response.

Council Member Goodman agreed to facilitate a meeting in the spring of 2002 between Minneapolis Public Works and CLPA. At the council member's request, the MPW staff had thoroughly researched right-of-way and land acquisition issues and had found out that, contrary to its earlier assessment, the off-road alignment might be feasible. Further, federal funds could in fact be reallocated to finish the trail within the old railroad corridor. The difference in cost between the two plans—one coming out of the corridor and

one staying in it—was approximately $700,000. Council Member
Goodman challenged CLPA to raise the money.

Shortly after the meeting with Council Member Goodman,
CLPA approached Minnesota State House Representative Margaret Anderson Kelliher. She was sympathetic to the proposal and
promised to work to secure state funding. It was soon apparent,
however, that more work would need to be done before the state
legislature could act.

### Creating an Alternative Alignment

CLPA needed to provide a viable alternative to the MPW plan. CLPA
contacted landscape architect Greg Brown and commissioned him
to sketch an alignment that ran along the BN* rail corridor (see *fig-*

*In 1996, the Burlington Northern Railroad merged with the Atchison, Topeka
and Santa Fe Railway to form the Burlington Northern and Santa Fe Railway
Company. In 2005 it was renamed the BNSF Railway. For simplicity's sake, Burlington Northern or BN will continue to be used in the text.

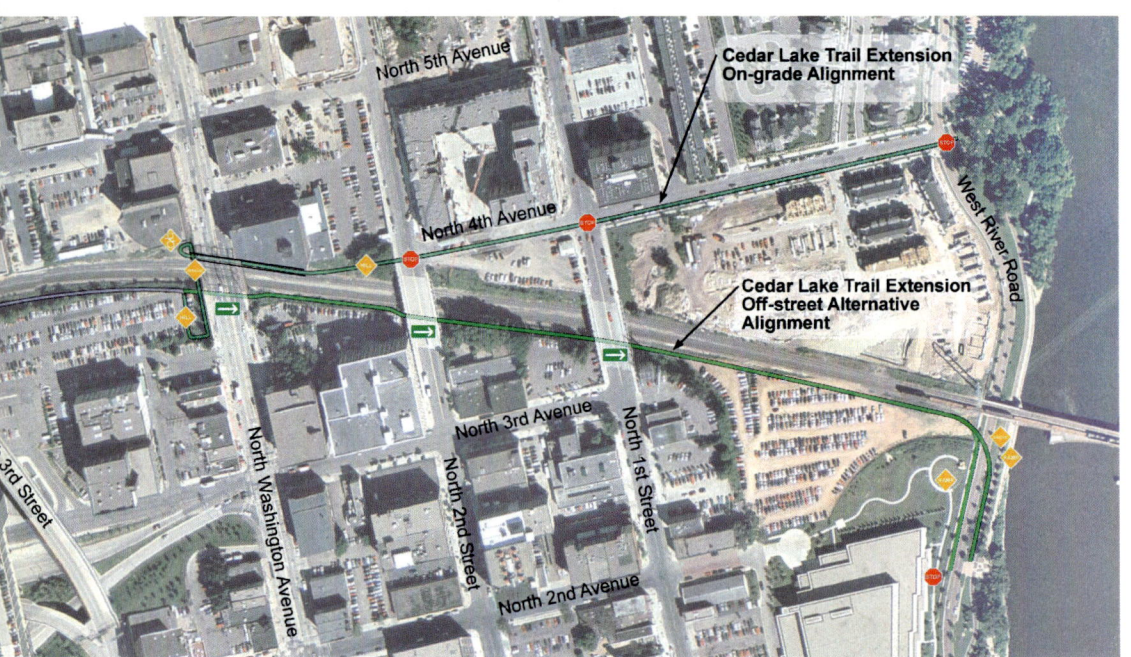

**FIGURE 34.** *Cedar Lake Trail Extension Off-street Alternative Alignment Map.*
Image courtesy of Greg Brown.

*ure 34*). CLPA cobbled together a narrative to go with it, as well as cost estimates. In the fall of 2002, CLPA began to shop this plan.[18]

### Finding Allies

CLPA began to build momentum. One member brokered a meeting with representatives from BN. Since its cooperation would be essential for any deal in the corridor, CLPA was eager to make sure that BN was onboard with the plan. Fortunately, BN voiced no objections. Meanwhile, CLPA raised awareness with local bike groups and advisory committees. As Minneapolis Bicycle Advisory Committee (BAC) member Billy Binder recalled, "I was convinced Public Works' plan was the way to go, that the obstacles were too great to overcome. But as I listened to the Cedar Lake Park Association's presentation before our BAC, I began to look at the situation with fresh eyes." CLPA began to generate a groundswell of public support, causing government officials to take notice.

Meanwhile, the situation had radically changed in the old Warehouse District. Whichever trail alignment was approved, it would have to run through the Minneapolis Warehouse District. As the new millennium dawned, this area was undergoing a tremendous transformation. Once a quiet backwater full of old storage buildings, the area now bustled with energy as developers renovated aging warehouse spaces and erected high-density housing units. Sleepy old Fourth Avenue, down which MPW had initially planned to paint a white stripe, was rapidly being transformed into a crowded thoroughfare lined with upscale condos. The area's neighborhood group did not favor a bike trail going right past their new homes. However, it *was* interested in trail access.

Meanwhile, another entity began to make its presence felt in the district: the Minnesota Ballpark Authority. It unveiled plans to build a new Twins baseball stadium right next to the BN rail corridor. The Warehouse District had become a very desirable place to be.

## Pitching the Proposal

In the three years following that fateful meeting with MPW, the Cedar Lake Park Association had put together a challenging alignment study and lobbied state and local entities to try to redirect the city's plan. It reached out to bicycle organizations. It also wrote articles.

Articles promoting the benefits of CLPA's trail alignment began appearing in the city's newspapers.[19] Slowly, CLPA had begun to shift the tone of the conversation: its "alternate alignment" now became the "preferred alignment." Neighborhood and bicycle advocacy groups took up the refrain. City leaders began to embrace the vision.

On April 14, 2003, one of CLPA's elder statesmen arranged a meeting with U.S. Congressman Martin Sabo. There, CLPA pitched a $3.4 million proposal for acquisition, design, and construction of the trail within the BN corridor. (This would be in addition to the money already allocated for Phase 3.) Congressman Sabo scanned the proposal, asked a few questions, and took his leave. The congressman's stoic demeanor and laconic comments did not fill the presenters with confidence, but his Chief-of-Staff Louis Moore told them to remain optimistic.

Later that month, several CLPA members spoke again with Representative Margaret Anderson Kelliher. The meeting with Congressman Sabo had ignited interest in the project and she committed to raising the necessary state match. That May, Hennepin County Commissioner Peter McLaughlin came out in favor of the preferred alignment. Since Hennepin County owned much of the land in the corridor, its support was critical. More and more it was becoming apparent: if the additional federal money came through, then CLPA's preferred alignment would receive the endorsement of state, county, and city officials.

In June, CLPA went back to see Minneapolis Council Member Lisa Goodman. She had been following the progress of the project and had heard from her constituents in the Warehouse District. She also expressed her approval of the preferred alignment. In light of the federal government's proposed increase in funding, the Minneapolis City Council directed MPW to reconsider CLPA's alignment.

### Providing a Land Survey

The 1989 Wirth Study had confirmed the feasibility of a trail that would run through downtown Minneapolis alongside the Burlington Northern corridor. CLPA's 2002 Alignment Proposal had updated and reinforced that initial finding. Now the city needed to know exactly what land it needed to acquire and what easement rights it needed to purchase before it could estimate project costs. Someone needed to pay for a detailed survey that would locate the section boundaries in the corridor. These section and quarter monuments had been obliterated over the previous century during the course of track realignment in the corridor. One CLPA member calculated that the work would cost at least $22,000. The CLPA steering committee debated funding the project. While some were in favor, others argued that funding such a survey would stretch the group's resources.

Luckily, the new Minnesota Ballpark Authority had a common boundary with the BN Railroad and it also needed detailed information about the corridor. Since Hennepin County had a considerable stake in the new stadium, it moved forward to complete the study. By the beginning of 2004, Hennepin County surveyors had located the lost monuments and provided the specifications needed for the Minnesota Ballpark Authority and city planners to move forward.

### Acquiring Funding

In the summer of 2003, one of the group's members invited Congressman James Oberstar to ride the Cedar Lake Regional Trail. During the ride he fell in with a few CLPA members who had been strategically placed along the trail. As a result of the impromptu trail meeting, Congressman Oberstar promised to work with his close friend Congressman Sabo to include the additional trail funding in the 2004 federal transportation bill. In March of 2004, CLPA's president received a late-night phone call from Congressman Sabo's chief of staff. "Does CLPA still want the money?" Louis Moore asked. "Of course we do!" And that was how funding for Phase III of the Cedar Lake Regional Trail to the Mississippi River got into U.S. HR 3550.

In April 2004, CLPA went to the state capitol to acquire a state match. The previous summer, CLPA had invited several lawmakers out to tour the trail. Now this outreach paid off. Securing authors from both sides of the aisle and both houses increased the chances for state funding. The group sensed victory . . . and then everything ground to a halt. Due to political infighting, there would be no federal transportation bill in 2004.

Undaunted, CLPA continued its campaign. In early 2005, one member contacted a friend of his who was a lobbyist for a construction conglomerate that bid on federal and state highway contracts. The lobbyist volunteered his expertise to expedite the process at both the federal and state level. He was tenacious. Once in a while, CLPA heard some rumblings from legislators that "their guy" was ruffling some feathers. CLPA apologized for any offence, but it knew that agitation often produced results.

Finally the long-delayed federal transportation bill became law in 2005. It included a provision for additional federal funds for the trail. As the Department of Public Works noted in its 2006 Request for City Council Action:

> The Cedar Lake Parkway [sic] Association, wishing to ensure the project's success, sought and received assistance from Congressman Sabo for additional federal funds. Their efforts were successful and in 2005 Congress allocated an additional $3 million for the project. This additional federal funding also required a significant local match. The City requested that the state provide the project $1.8 million for the local match as part of their 2006 Bonding Bill. The Minnesota Legislature approved this funding and it is now available.[20]

### The Cost of Completing the Trail to the River

Due to the long delay, what began in 2001 as a $700,000 gap in a $6 million project had become by 2006 a $10 million package of federal and state aid. It was a high price to pay to complete a plan proposed almost twenty years earlier. To those who criticized the trail as costly and trivial, CLPA replied that land acquisition in the downtown area of a major metropolitan area *was* expensive, but the payoff will be enormous. Commuters will have access to downtown businesses. University students will be able to bicycle to school. Recreational users will loop the north and south metro areas using the Grand Rounds bisected by the Cedar Lake Regional Trail (the realization of the *Figure 8*). Thousands of people, including young children, will be able to travel through the heart of a downtown metropolitan area without encountering one motor vehicle. No other city in North America could make that claim. Costly? Yes, but hardly trivial.

To attain its goal, the Cedar Lake Park Association built bridges to community groups and persuaded all levels of government to embrace its vision of an off-road bicycle and pedestrian trail through the heart of a major metropolitan area. It brokered meetings and wrote articles. It funded studies and sponsored tours. And it doggedly followed Winston Churchill's admonition to "Never, never, never give up."

### Spring 2011

Finally, after a decade of planning, construction on the trail to the river began in the summer of 2010. City engineers had hoped to finish the trail to the river by the fall, but delays forced them to shut down for the winter. On April 15, 2011, construction started up again.

One April morning in 2011, a passing bicyclist caught a hazy shot of construction workers creating a cement structure to stabilize the road bed next to the trail: one of the last pieces in finishing the trail.

One person wrote an article about the day he first rode the trail:

As I rode my bicycle through downtown Minneapolis this morning, the aroma of fresh tar wafted through the air. My nose led me to the construction area of the Cedar Lake Trail—the final section between First Street North and West River Parkway. And there . . . was a sight to behold.

The trail was paved.

Today, Tuesday, May 24, 2011, should be remembered as the day, to borrow Abraham Lincoln's wonderful phrasing, "the Cedar

**FIGURE 35.** Final construction on the trail to the river, April 2011. Image courtesy of CLPA.

Lake Trail flows unvexed to the Father of Waters." Although there is still some work to be done (fencing along the stretch between First Street and The Fed) and the gate is still closed to the west, the final section of the Cedar Lake Regional Trail to the Mississippi River is complete.[21]

On June 14, 2011, the city held the ribbon-cutting ceremony marking the official opening of the Cedar Lake Regional Trail to the Mississippi River. The rain held off long enough for a brief round of speeches by city and county officials as they gathered on the banks of the river across from the eastern trailhead. Mayor R. T. Rybak spoke glowingly of riding from downtown Minneapolis out to the Cedar Lake prairie. He went on to say, "Citizens' groups like the Cedar Lake Park Association hold [public officials'] feet to the fire, to make sure projects like this get done."[22] As the rain began to fall, many bicyclists scampered home using the trail for the first time.

Some issues still exist. As the trail exits the Federal Reserve property at the east end of the trail, users will need to cross the busy West River Parkway to access the river road trail. CLPA is advocating a flyover bridge for the future, so that users need not encounter vehicles. For now, bicyclists, pedestrians, and motorists need to be cautious at the crossing. Access from the trail to downtown streets is limited and needs to be enhanced. More public transit could make its way into the corridor; if so, the trail may need to be realigned. Safety continues to be an issue along the corridor, especially at night.

Eventually the trail will cross the river and directly connect to the University of Minnesota, the Minneapolis Northwest Diagonal, and the Gateway State Trail up to the Willard Munger State Trail in Duluth. To the west the trail already runs through St. Louis Park and Hopkins and connects to trails that run to Chaska, Excelsior, and as far as Hutchinson—ninety miles away. Perhaps, in the future, it could reach across the country.

CLPA will continue to advocate measures to maintain the trail's reputation as the premier nonmotorized commuter and recreational trail system in the nation.

**FIGURE 36.** Fall planting in the Cedar Lake Park Prairie. Image courtesy of CLPA.

# 9

## The Prairie

A TALLGRASS PRAIRIE ONCE DOMINATED THE MINNESOTA LAND-scape. In the late 1800s, settlers began plowing the prairieland into farmland. By 1960, less than one percent of the state's original prairie remained. Since then, conservation efforts have been underway throughout the state to bring back the native prairie.

Cedar Lake Park's Concept Master Plan specified restoring the area north of Cedar Lake to its original state as a tallgrass prairie. In 1995, the city of Minneapolis and the Minneapolis Park Board contracted Prairie Restorations, Inc., to site-match (that is, select the appropriate plants for the soil conditions) and prepare the newly contoured land. Using a seed drill for the grasses and a broadcast spreader for the flower seeds, the contractor carefully planted the newly contoured area with native prairie grasses and flowers.

As the prairie began to evolve, a variety of grasses started dominate, especially big bluestem—a native plant that imbues the prairie with a purple hue when it matures in the fall (see *figure 36*). Since the grasses had taken hold so successfully, CLPA—under the supervision of the Minneapolis Park Board—supplemented the original planting by sowing select areas of the prairie with over 14,000 seedlings of native flowers.

The prairie did have a number of invasive plants, especially a large outcropping of leafy spurge. CLPA volunteers take special precautions when eradicating this toxic plant (see *figure 37*). MPRB has also released a bio-control to contain the leafy spurge.

After a decade of growth, CLPA commissioned a scientific survey to monitor the health of the prairie. In 2005, Joe Schmitz, In-

**FIGURE 37.** Volunteers use rubber gloves while eradicating leafy spurge. Image courtesy of CLPA.

structor of Environmental Studies and Minnesota Natural History at Normandale College, led a team out into the field to observe and measure the prairie plant community. Using GPS technology, the team identified survey plots within the prairie. As he noted in his 2005 report, "The identification and record of the location of the various species found will serve as a baseline for further observation over time."

CLPA invited Schmitz to return to the Cedar Lake Park prairie restoration site in September 2011. Although he had walked the prairie many times in the intervening five years simply to enjoy the ever-changing habitat, he came this time with a specific goal: to revisit the survey plots recorded in 2005 and to assess efforts to restore the Cedar Lake Park prairie by documenting the changes in the natural community. (The updated Prairie Transect Survey is available on the CLPA website.) Here is his report.

# Report on the Progress
## *of the*
## Cedar Lake Park Prairie: 2011

The prairie continues to develop and flourish. Native grasses are well established on the site, with big blue stem, Indian grass, and little blue stem asserting their natural dominance in the prairie community. I was pleased to see prairie cord grass, among my personal favorites, thriving in some of the seasonally wetter areas. These native grasses are constantly building soil through their growth and decomposition, slowly improving conditions for other plants to follow.

Many of the wildflowers are also showing their true colors. Areas that once held a few individuals now hold many; wild bergamot and purple and white prairie clover are three species of note. Other wildflowers such as lead plant, butterfly milkweed, blazing star, partridge pea, and round-head bush clover are wide spread throughout the prairie.

With the exceptions of sweet clover, spotted knapweed (historically linked to railroads for their distribution), and common mullein, even the invasive non-native species seem to be losing ground to the natives. Common mullein—with upright cigar-like 3–6 foot long stems and seed heads—though invasive, are not necessarily bad. As they die back and decompose they add nutrients to the soils, and will themselves eventually be replaced by native species more suited to the improved soils. As a whole the prairie community continues to thrive.

As the plant community continues to develop, so too does the community of animals associated with it. In addition to the guild of pollinators noted in years past, herbivorous and predatory insects, spiders, and soil-dwelling organisms have definitely found the habitat to their liking. Blister beetles, Pennsylvania soldier beetles, numerous grasshopper species, and black and yellow agriope spiders were commonly encountered. Other animals observed, either directly or through their sign, include white-tail deer, red fox, ground squirrels, garter snakes and American toads. American goldfinches and gray catbirds, along with migratory white-throated and white-crowned sparrows were common companions as I conducted the survey.

The prairie is growing both as habitat and community, its benefits not only measurable in terms of environment for native plant species and their associates, but also as a resource for a suite of other species. Of equal importance is the prairie's value as a resource for uplifting the human spirit, as visitors to the park and travelers through it consciously or unconsciously reconnect with nature.

*A detailed list of plants recorded in the Cedar Lake Park Prairie in 2011 is available in Appendix E.*

### Partnering in the Prairie

Under the guidance of Park Board staff, CLPA continues to remove invasive plants such as spotted knapweed and wormwood and eradicate volunteer Russian elms and cottonwood saplings. A dedicated group of prairie lovers constantly watches over it, reporting any activities that may impact the prairie.

In the fall of 2011, CLPA members met with MPRB Commissioner Anita Tabb and Assistant Superintendent for Planning Services Bruce Chamberlain. Since the Park Board recently had a significant change in leadership, CLPA wanted to acquaint them with role that CLPA has played in the development of the prairie and the historic partnership that MPRB and CLPA have had in its management. CLPA presented copies of the Cedar Lake Park Concept Master Plan and the group discussed prairie management issues such as burning, mowing, and planting. The renewed partnership plans to meet again and establish a prairie management protocol for future activities in the prairie.

**FIGURE 38.** Installing the Cedar Lake Park Memorial Grove Bench. Image courtesy of Meredith Montgomery.

A few winters after its creation, a small group met in the Frank Lloyd Wright–designed house on the southeast shore of Cedar Lake to discuss enhancing the Cedar Lake Park Memorial Grove. Many thought it would be appropriate to have a place of respite within the grove. One member sketched a design for a simple bench that evoked the spirit of the place. Another offered to underwrite the project. In the winter of 2003, with the Park Board's approval, volunteers placed the Cedar Lake Park Memorial Grove Bench in the grove. Made of dolomite sandstone, the rough-cut top of the bench ripples slightly, evoking the contour of the prairie beyond. Like much of park, it's a little difficult to get to, but it's worth the hike.

# 10
## Still Here

EVERY YEAR AT THE CEDAR LAKE PARK ANNUAL RETREAT, THE GROUP asks itself if it still has value. Is its mission still viable? Every year the group feels the need to justify its existence. Outlined in this chapter are some challenges CLPA still faces.

### The Mound

The Cedar (Indian) Mound at the north end of the lake needs attention. In 2007, CLPA commissioned a document, the Mound at Cedar Lake Concept Plan. Drawing from the organization's master plan, the mound plan sought to increase access to this area. The design proposed improving the health of the area by eradicating non-native species and restoring disturbed areas. The first step in the plan would be getting rid of buckthorn. Buckthorn is aggressive and pernicious—returning again and again—so this cannot be a one-time project, but must be an ongoing process. CLPA will need to find the funds to execute the plan and oversee maintenance.

### The Cedar Lake Park Memorial Grove

In its earliest days, as part of its fundraising effort, SCLP ran a campaign to create the Cedar Lake Park Memorial Grove (informally known as the Cedar Grove). Members could purchase red cedar trees that would be planted in a double-spiral pattern in the heart of the Cedar Lake woodlands. More than sixty members donated to the memorial.

**FIGURE 39.** Volunteers enjoy the bench at Cedar Lake Park Memorial Grove. Image courtesy of Meredith Montgomery.

In October of 1996, over one hundred friends and family gathered for a ceremonial planting of the first six trees. Eventually CLPA volunteers planted sixty-five cedars in the grove. Several dedicated volunteers maintain the grove, periodically bushwhacking buckthorn and other exotics that threaten to choke the young cedars. Over the years, a few of the trees have died and members have transplanted volunteer cedars from the surrounding area to maintain the spirals.

CLPA has struggled with a continuing challenge, however. Along with planting trees, the group had pledged to post the names of those who were being honored or memorialized. Some donors expected, not unreasonably, that the signage would be posted *somewhere in the grove*. CLPA has debated how to fulfill this promise without violating one of its core precepts: minimizing human artifacts in the park. The MPRB has also weighed in, reminding CLPA that it has a policy to discourage signage on trees in its parks. Though CLPA considered several options, such as pavers, none seemed to fit.

However, evolving technology has supplied a solution. CLPA is adding a page to its website that will serve as a virtual Cedar Grove Memorial. Donors will be able to post missives about those they wish to honor. In this way, CLPA will be able to fulfill the spirit of its original pledge.

### Honoring a Debt

Several years ago, former Minneapolis & St. Louis Railway workers earmarked a small donation to the park. The donors wished to commemorate the history of the local railroad and its shops and yards that once lay between Cedar Lake and the Kenwood Hills. The rail legacy influenced the development of the Bryn Mawr and Kenwood communities. CLPA has struggled to honor its commitment without violating its principle to minimize human artifacts in the park. Solving this challenge has become intertwined with strategies to influence the development of light-rail transit in the park.

### Southwest LRT

If the Southwest Light Rail Transitway (Southwest LRT) is constructed, it will run through the Kenilworth corridor on the east side of Cedar Lake. It will dramatically affect Greater Cedar Lake Park. (Greater Cedar Lake Park comprises all the land surrounding Cedar Lake north to the Bryn Mawr Bluff and east to the Kenwood Bluff.) In 2008, CLPA developed a statement of design principles concerning how the Southwest LRT should relate to the adjacent park and trails.

1. Safeguard human life, protect the water quality in Cedar Lake, and enhance wildlife habitat, habitat connectivity, and quality of the natural environment.
2. Minimize any negative impact on people's experience of Cedar Lake Park and the park-like surrounding areas.
3. Maintain neighborhood and regional access to Cedar Lake Park, Cedar Lake Regional Trail, the Kenilworth Trail, and the Midtown Greenway.

4. Minimize the intrusiveness of permanent and temporal changes to the environment of Cedar Lake Park and the park-like surrounding areas.

5. Mitigate unavoidable changes in the environment with investments that provide exceptional value to the goal of "Nurturing Nature."

6. Wherever the LRT is not tunneled in the corridor, enhance the LRT riders' positive experience of Cedar Lake Park and the surrounding park-like areas as they pass through the corridor.

7. Design any and all stations that are adjacent to Cedar Lake Park in such a way that they are compatible with a park-like setting—like a park lodge or park ranger's station.

As a member of Hennepin County's Southwest LRT Planning Advisory Committee, CLPA was able to append these principles to the committee's findings. Several members also obtained seats on MPRB's Southwest LRT Citizens' Advisory Committee. With this representation, CLPA hopes to communicate the wishes of the community concerning issues related to construction of light rail in the Cedar Lake area. CLPA's main objectives are to protect Greater Cedar Lake Park and the Kenilworth and Cedar Lake trails.

In the fall of 2010, CLPA sponsored a design charrette. It invited several noted landscape architects, including Roger Martin and John Koepke from the University of Minnesota. After an overview of the project and a walk of the area, the landscape architects spent the day sketching designs of intersections and transit stations in the Cedar Lake area. CLPA then fashioned a narrative and, along with the charrette sketches, created a booklet which was distributed to decision-makers at all levels of government. CLPA's goal is to create a framework for the upcoming station-area designs and for the flow of the Cedar Lake Regional Trail as it intersects with the Southwest LRT in the Cedar Lake area (see *figure 40*).

*We need an underpass* beneath the light rail line.
*This would respect the integrity of the Trail, ensure safety, promote connectivity, and may even increase usage.*

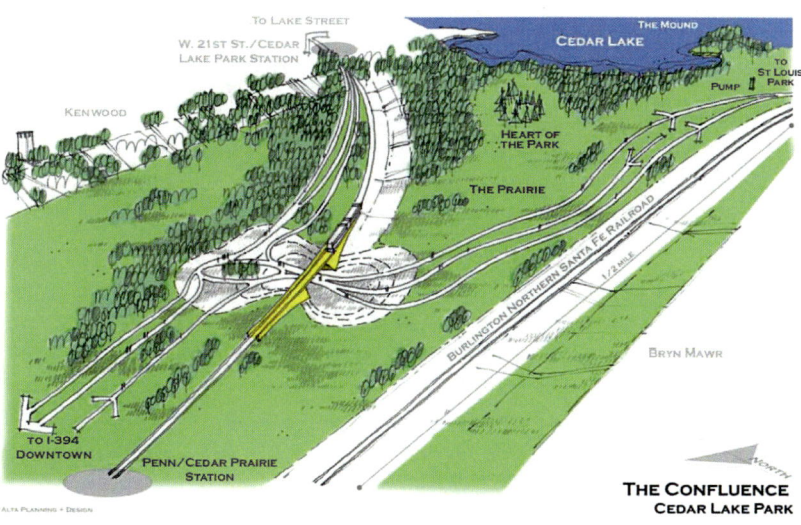

**FIGURE 40.** Drawing of a grade-separated intersection of the Cedar Lake Regional Trail and the Southwest LRT, 2011. Illustration courtesy of Steve Durrant.

### Stewarding Hidden Beach

Members of CLPA have long taken an interest in Hidden Beach, the area on the lake's eastern shore near 21st Street and Upton Avenue. The area has a long history of recreational use. Up to the beginning of the twentieth century, Cedar Lake was considerably larger and contained a large, shallow east bay. Along the shore of the bay, dockhands serviced a fleet of boats. Blue-collar families rode the Minneapolis & St. Louis Railway out from the city and spent their weekends boating or fishing in what was then considered a country lake.

With the drop in the water level of the lake in the early 1900s, the bay dried up and the area became a backwater attracting freespirited individuals who flocked to a secluded beach via a hidden path through dense undergrowth. By the 1970s, the isolated beach encouraged a bohemian lifestyle (the area was also known as Nude Beach). The word spread, and folks streamed in to enjoy the 24-hour scene that included drumming, dancing, and bonfires through the night. Since the beachgoers tended to keep to themselves, authorities often overlooked the uninhibited behavior there.

Beginning in the early 1990s, members of CLPA began work to enhance the natural environment of the area. Volunteers placed rocks and logs to guide people through the area and away from the newly introduced native plants in the area.

Eventually, the beach culture became so popular, and the boisterous activities of the crowds so excessive, that during the course of several scorching summers, the large parties aroused neighborhood outrage. They demanded that the city and MPRB act. In 2003, to the dismay of many beach users, MPRB foresters eradicated the buckthorn understory, making the beach area visible from the road. While the action upset some, others welcomed the visual access to the lake. In any case, within a few years the vegetation grew back and the culture of permissiveness returned.

In 2008, MPRB asserted active management control by opening a gravel road access, bringing in sand to reinforce the heavily-eroded shoreline, staffing newly erected lifeguard towers and picnic areas, and increasing park police presence. They officially designated the area East Cedar Lake Beach. Despite all of this, not that much has changed. Hidden Beach remains a secluded place where people can engage with nature and each other. CLPA continues to actively monitor the area, acting as a bridge from the beach community to the Park Board and the surrounding neighborhoods.

With MPRB's approval, CLPA has coordinated hundreds of projects within the park over the past twenty years. As part of its mission to *provide opportunities for people to learn to live in community with nature and one another*, the group has afforded educational opportunities for grade school classes, scout troops, bird-watching enthusiasts, and alumni clubs. The photographs over the next few pages show just a few of the activities overseen by CLPA.

**FIGURE 41 (top).** Kids explore flora and fauna in the open-air classroom at the park. Image courtesy of CLPA.

**FIGURE 42 (bottom).** Girl Scouts clearing buckthorn in the park take a break. Photo by Meredith Montgomery.

**FIGURE 43 (top).** Young volunteer cutting down buckthorn. Image courtesy of Meredith Montgomery.

**FIGURE 44 (bottom).** Wood chipping around the Cedar Lake shoreline. Image courtesy of Meredith Montgomery.

**Still Here**

As we enter a period of increased budget constraints, the Cedar Lake Park Association believes it still has a significant role to play in active stewardship of the park and trail it has worked so hard to establish. Indeed, the role of local citizens in maintaining parks and trails has become even more critical. So, as CLPA moves into its third decade of existence, it still believes its mission has relevance.

Those who campaigned to save Cedar Lake Park created a legacy greater than a new park or trail. They demonstrated how creating an urban nature park can connect human, plant, and animal communities and help generate sustainable cities. They envisioned a trail as a linear park, a green-ribbon necklace connecting the treasures of the city. They demonstrated how ordinary citizens can empower themselves and develop new strategies to interact with government agencies to get projects done. And it all started with a piece of land that people felt passionate about.

After all, who doesn't love a park?

**FIGURE 45.** Bicyclists head east on the Cedar Lake Regional Trail. Image courtesy of Meredith Montgomery.

# Save Cedar Lake Park

## Organizational Guidelines

1. **CREATE THE VISION.** Be bold in doing so. Base it on values and need. Be positive. Be "for something" rather than "against something".

2. **DEFINE THE VISION IN BROAD TERMS.** Avoid specific design details. Without agreement on a broad vision, trying to get agreement on specific details often divides a group. Agreement regarding the values, need and vision will raise the probabilities of working out the design details over time.

3. **CLAIM, NAME AND SAVE.** Claim the land for the highest and best use. Name it in light of this use. Save it for this use.

4. **COMMUNICATE THE VISION, THE VALUES AND THE NEED.** Nurture Nature! Communicate the message over and over, over and over. Never stop!

5. **USE GRAPHICS, VISIBLE SYMBOLS TO KEEP PROJECT IN PEOPLE'S AWARENESS.** Maps, billboards, buttons, T-shirts, photos, etc.

6. **ENROLL PEOPLE INTO THE VISION.** Be broad based. Enroll citizens. You can never have too many citizens enrolled in the Vision. Politicians who are leaders will see the value of the vision and will join in leading the project. Other politicians will join the efforts when they see large numbers of citizens supporting the project.

7. **MAKE FRIENDS. AVOID CONFRONTATION.** Everyone is a potential supporter. It takes more time for some to understand the need, appreciate the values and catch the vision.

8. **INVITE EVERYONE TO JOIN THE ORGANIZATION.** Keep membership simple.

9. **INVITE PEOPLE WITH IDEAS, ENERGY, SPECIAL TALENTS OR ABILITIES TO JOIN THE STEERING COMMITTEE.** Steering Committee is open. Size of committee and length of service by an individual vary depending on need, interest and availability.

10. **WORK THROUGH IDEAS AND PLANS UNTIL THERE IS CONSENSUS,** especially in the Steering Committee and the Board. If a consensus is not possible, have a very high majority in agreement before taking action.

11. **ALL BOARD MEMBERS PARTICIPATE IN THE STEERING COMMITTEE.** Board ratifies decisions which need to be ratified for legal purposes.

12. **COORDINATE ALL ACTIVITIES THROUGH THE STEERING COMMITTEE.** The Chair of the Board is also Chair of the Steering Committee.

13. CREATE SPECIFIC TASK COMMITTEES. e.g. legal, communications, fund raising, concert, etc. These committee are created by the Steering Committee.

14. INVITE AND ENCOURAGE PERSONS OF UNIQUE GIFTS OR RESOURCES TO MAKE SIGNIFICANT CONTRIBUTIONS TO THE PROJECT.

15. ASK PERSONS WITH SPECIAL CONNECTIONS TO CONTACT OTHERS AND ASK THEM TO MAKE A SIGNIFICANT CONTRIBUTION TO THE PROJECT.

16. HOLD PUBLIC EVENTS TO RAISE AWARENESS AND INVOLVE PEOPLE IN THE PROJECT. Examples: clean ups, a concert, nature walks through the property, acquisition party, etc.

17. RAISE FUNDS FROM THE PRIVATE SECTOR AS A STIMULUS FOR PUBLIC SECTOR MATCHING FUNDS.

18. CREATE PARTNERSHIPS AND STRATEGIC ALLIANCES WITH OTHER ORGANIZATIONS. Have other organizations endorse and promote the project and give them credit for doing so.

19. ESTABLISH A SPECIAL RELATIONSHIP, MARKED BY SHARED DECISION-MAKING REGARDING ALL ASPECTS OF THE PROJECT, WITH THE PARK BOARD.

20. EDUCATE AND BE VISIBLY PRESENT TO GOVERNMENTAL LEADERS OF THE CITY, REGION AND STATE. The best education is through experience. Get as many leaders to experience the actual place of the project, the video, the slide presentation, brochures with maps, the newsletter, etc..

21. INVOLVE THE MEDIA, neighborhood news papers, TV, radio, metro wide new papers, etc. Have updates and special coverage at crucial times.

22. HOLD THE VISION! COMPLETE THE MISSION! ONE STEP AT A TIME!

23. CELEBRATE THE PROCESS AS WELL AS SUCCESSFUL OUTCOMES!

24. BE WILLING TO WORK HARD. STICK WITH IT. HANG IN THERE.

25. APPRECIATE EACH OTHER. LEARN FROM EACH OTHER. MAKE SOME NEW FRIENDS. HAVE FUN! LAUGH A LOT! ENJOY THE PROCESS!

# Appendix B.
# Statement of Philosophy

## CEDAR LAKE PARK AND TRAILS

*Citizens' Advisory Committee*

## STATEMENT OF PHILOSOPHY,
Opportunity, Purpose, Timetable, Objectives
& Design Principles

### PHILOSOPHY

As people of the earth, we are part of an interdependent community of air, soil, water, plants and animals. For life, we depend on clean air, drinkable water, nutritious food, healing remedies, protective clothing and adequate shelter. To enrich our lives, we need to experience nature's breadth and beauty, power and poetry, mystery and majesty.

We must respect, protect and nurture nature in all its diversity. Failure to do so, directly and indirectly leads to the degradation of our life support system, threatening life's quality and our very survival.

With more stress being imposed upon natural ecosystems by increasing urbanization and short-sighted planning, our future will depend on redeveloping cities which function more harmoniously with nature. Towards that end, it is vitally important to preserve and expand natural areas within existing cities where citizens can directly experience nature and its rhythms and cycles.

Through personal encounters with nature and reflective learning, we increase our appreciation of nature's ways and humanity's role in the web of life. These experiences refresh our spirits, strengthen our bond with all living beings, and remind us of the impact of our individual and collective decisions. Aware of nature's gifts, we need to ever renew our commitment to nurture nature locally and work for a sustainable, global community.

## MINNEAPOLIS, MINNESOTA

## OPPORTUNITY

Seldom is there an opportunity to reclaim a large tract of land in the center of a major metropolitan area, create a nature preserve and develop a compatible trail system for non-motorized transportation. When the opportunity occurs, it must be seized and made a reality.

To meet such a challenge, it is vital for individuals, business, government, institutions and organizations to work together at unprecedented levels of service, commitment and cooperation. When these partnerships unite in efforts to improve the quality of life and the liveability of our communities, we see the world as it can truly be.

Cedar Lake Park with its connecting trails is a unique opportunity to transform our urban landscape and the way a city functions. To create a nature park with a variety of ecological communities and trails in the heart of the city provides real hope for a new vision for the future. With a significant land base now secured, the challenge of Cedar Lake Park and Trails must be met through a sensitive and creative design.

## PARTNERSHIP

Strong, independent citizen action, carried out in concert with the Park Board, has made Cedar Lake Park and connecting trails possible. The continuation of this broad-based, independent citizen involvement in the design, development and governance of the park and trails is essential if Cedar Lake Park is to realize its full potential. Continuing to build on past cooperative efforts, this new level of partnership — marked by shared decision-making by citizens, the Park Board and other public agencies — will assure the realization and future preservation of the vision/purpose of the park and trails.

## PURPOSE

Our purpose is to establish and manage a harmonious community of soil, water, plants, wildlife, and people while providing access for people to experience the park and to travel by trail throughout the region by non-polluting forms of transportation.

## TIMETABLE

Although the existing land surrounding Cedar Lake and the newly acquired tracts appear wild and natural, nearly every portion has been significantly disturbed over the last century. Left to purely natural processes, this land cannot regain its full potential. While the beginning stages of restoration will require more active and noticeable management, natural processes will be the primary element of change throughout this long-term plan. We envision that the development of this sanctuary will continue well into the next century and be sustained thereafter.

## OBJECTIVES

To realize the promise and challenge of creating and sustaining a nature conservancy and connecting trail system in the center of an urban area, objectives must be clearly stated. As the Citizens' Advisory Committee, we submit the following objectives for Cedar Lake Park and Trails:

* **PROTECT** and improve the water resources and soils.

* **RECONSTITUTE** a variety of native plant communities which reflect lake, wetland, prairie, savannah, woodland and forest ecosystems.

* **MANAGE** the plant and animal communities for their long-term integrity, stability and beauty.

* **CONNECT** ecosystems, green corridors, and trail systems.

* **MINIMIZE** human artifacts and amenities within the conservancy area.

* **INTEGRATE** the surrounding land and land uses to complement and enhance the park.

* **FACILITATE** experiences in which people learn about nature and gain greater appreciation for humanity's role in the web of life.

* **CELEBRATE** people living in harmony with nature and each other.

# DESIGN PRINCIPLES

Through the process of identifying, discussing and refining all of the considerations for the park and trail, a series of design principles have evolved. Organized within the framework of the aforementioned objectives, these principles have been developed to guide, not dictate, the specific design of the park and ensure ongoing citizen involvement in the use and development of the park and trail. As the Citizens Advisory Committee, we submit the following as the design principles for Cedar Lake Park and Trail:

**PROTECT and improve the water resource and soils.**

* Alter the existing topography and soils in those areas where modifications will reduce/eliminate erosion and improve the soil conditions necessary for establishing native plant communities or to otherwise create/improve park amenities.

* Consider features with historical or cultural significance as park amenities to be incorporated into the overall design.

* Improve the quality of water entering Cedar Lake by increasing the vegetative buffer along the shoreline (except for currently established beaches), by minimizing impervious surfaces where direct runoff into the lake is likely to occur, and by other appropriate methods.

RECONSTITUTE a variety of native plant communities which reflect lake, wetland, prairie, savannah, woodland and forest ecosystems.

* Convert and maintain the large open expanse to the north and northeast of Cedar Lake primarily as Oak Savannah (native prairie grasses, flowers and scattered oak trees).

* Manage the upland areas currently containing mature oak trees primarily as Oak Woodlands with prairie openings.

* Convert and maintain the remaining forested areas and other areas not suitable for savannah or prairie to Maple Basswood Forest with other native tree and shrub species scattered among this community.

* Enhance and expand the wetland communities along the lakeshore particularly in those locations where storm water runoff is most likely to occur.

* Reestablish/establish additional wetlands (ephemeral ponds, wet meadows, marshes and/or streams), based upon historic evidence and the suitability of the topography and soils to the extent possible.

* Plant Red Cedar trees as individuals or in small groupings in the drier portions of the park and along the commuter trail corridor(s).

* Plant White Cedar and Tamarack trees near the lakeshore.

MANAGE the plant and animal communities for their long term integrity, stability and beauty.

* Emphasize natural succession in implementing the transition from undesired to desired vegetative species.

* Utilize integrated pest management principles and minimal chemical use to control disease and exotic species, reconstitute native plant communities, or otherwise maintain the desired plant and animal communities.

* Maximize habitat edges to encourage wildlife diversity.

* Retain a significant number of dead trees unless they are endangering visitor safety, park facilities or harboring harmful insects and/or disease.

* Conduct authorized burning for land management objectives.

* Increase selected wildlife populations by providing songbird feeding stations and artificial nesting structures.

* Consider a transitional area on marginal sites within the park/trail corridor for an unleashed dog exercise area. Established ordinances as they pertain to dogs and other domestic animals will be enforced in other areas.

* Use low-impact, non-motorized maintenance practices to the extent possible.

CONNECT ecosystems, green corridors and trail systems.

* Link all types of trails in and through the park to provide a variety of compatible experiences and uses for both park visitors and commuter trail users.

* Extend green (wildlife) corridors and non-motorized trails from Cedar Lake Park and Trails to connect non-contiguous parks and natural areas.

MINIMIZE human artifacts and amenities in the conservancy area.

* Restrict buildings (including restrooms and information kiosks) to designated entrances and/or along the outside perimeter of the conservancy with sensitivity to neighborhood concerns.

* Consider the use of vegetation or materials which appear natural as barriers to reduce noise and light from entering the conservancy area.

* Restrict artificial lighting to designated park entrances and along the commuter bike trail at the lowest level possible without compromising a high level of commuter trail usage.

* Locate the most conspicuous signage, in a style reflective of this park, at the designated entrances and/or along the park perimeter.

* Design interpretive signage for the interior of the park to be unobtrusive and long lasting.

* Provide trail location markers and means for emergency communication.

* Develop rest areas and points of interest which are reflective of the park, sensitive to the topography and constructed primarily of natural materials.

* Encourage the use of natural materials, including vegetation, for any required barriers with special consideration for wildlife movement and the necessary duration for such barriers.

* Provide solid waste and recycling containers at designated entrances, heavily used sites and along the commuter trail corridor(s).

* Restrict the use of motorized vehicles (except wheelchairs) from the interior of the park except for emergency purposes and/or required maintenance activities.

* Remove human artifacts which are not considered park amenities.

INTEGRATE the surrounding land and land uses to complement and enhance the park.

* Maintain and/or improve existing sites and create new sites which provide significant vistas within the park or of the surrounding area (including the downtown skyline) with sensitivity to neighborhood considerations.

* Create transition experiences for the designated park entrances and selected neighborhood access points.

* Disperse designated entrances along the main transportation routes.

* Emphasize public transportation and non-motorized vehicles as the primary means for accessing the park with small, dispersed parking areas located adjacent to or near the park.

* Locate commuter bike trails and associated amenities along the park perimeter and encourage these trail users to visit and experience the park interior on foot.

* Develop and implement a "best management plan" for the watersheds contributing surface water to Cedar Lake.

* Extend the reconstitution of native plant communities to lands adjacent to the park and trail corridor including existing park land, railroad right-of-way and willing private property owners.

* Develop protocol for identifying and evaluating potential acquisition parcels.

* Develop cooperative agreements for existing and future adjacent land owners which includes such things as land trusts and covenants.

**FACILITATE** experiences in which people learn about nature and gain greater appreciation for humanity's role in the web of life.

✳ Provide a variety of interpretive experiences and materials focusing on the natural resources, history, and current and future management plans for the park.

✳ Establish an interior pedestrian-oriented trail system which:

* respects topographical features, plant communities and designated wildlife preserves.

* provides access to the most important features of the park by balancing visual interest, the sense of solitude and the need for safety.

* provides representative park experiences and highlighted features for physically disabled visitors.

* provides limited access by motorized emergency and maintenance vehicles.

* facilitates both hiking and cross country skiing.

* excludes bicycles and in-line skates and seriously consider the temporary exception of mountain bikes on the hilly, highly filled area on the east side of Cedar Lake and limited access to that site until an area can be developed for mountain biking in some other location.

✳ Encourage Park Police to be on foot or other non-motorized means while providing protection, law enforcement and interpretive opportunities for park and trail visitors.

**CELEBRATE** people living in harmony with nature and each other.

✳ Create, use and make available graphics of the park and trails which symbolize a harmonious relationship between people and nature.

✳ Create opportunities for people of all ages, backgrounds and cultures to actively participate in educational programs, management activities and other related service projects.

✳ Plan a variety of events which bring people together in and on behalf of the park and the trail.

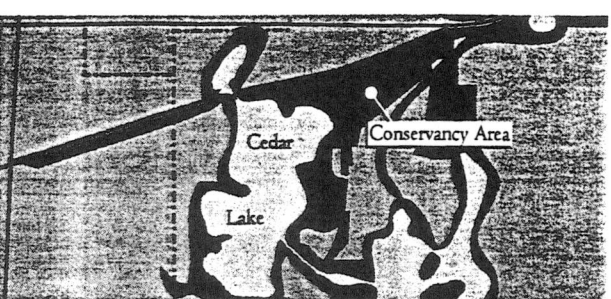

*The conservancy area is defined as the entire corridor between Highway 100 and the Cedar Lake Parkway bridge and the land bordered by the Burlington Northern Railroad right-of-way between Cedar Lake Parkway bridge and the leased Hennepin County Rail Authority land on the north; the shoreline of Cedar Lake from the Cedar Lake Parkway bridge to the Kenilworth Canal; around the private properties along Burnham Boulevard and Washburn Avenues on the south; and the park boundary, including the leased Hennepin County Rail Authority land on the east.*

Signed, this 1st day of March, 1993,
by the members of the Cedar Lake Park and Trails Citizens' Advisory Committee:

# Appendix C.
# Timeline of Activities
# 1970–2011

**1970s and 1980s**

In the 1970s, Burlington Northern (BN) removes yards north of Cedar Lake

In 1984, Chicago & North Western Railway razes workshops northeast of Cedar Lake

Old rail yards revert to prairie and woodlands

**1989**

BNSF decides to sell land north of Cedar Lake

In March, city holds public meeting to discuss use of land

In April, citizens form "Save Cedar Lake Park" (SCLP)

Minneapolis Mayor Don Fraser endorses SCLP vision

Minneapolis Parks & Recreation Board (MPRB) embraces Cedar Lake Park concept

MPRB establishes Cedar Lake Park Citizens' Advisory Committee (CAC)

MPRB commissions Wirth Design Associates to study feasibility of connecting Cedar Lake Park with the Mississippi River

Wirth Study concludes park and corridor are feasible

SCLP sells "Nurture Nature" T-shirts and "Save Cedar Lake Park" buttons to raise funds

In December, SCLP publishes first edition of *Save Cedar Lake Park Update* newsletter

## 1990

SCLP commits to raising one-third of the funds needed to acquire land

Key civic leaders and legislators pledge support

Metropolitan Council approves addition of park to Regional Park Master Plan

SCLP receives a Neighborhood Environmental Award

Green-and-white Save Cedar Lake Park buttons sprout up at state legislature

SCLP envisions Cedar Lake Regional Trail turning the Grand Rounds into a "Figure Eight"

Major donors pledge $335,000 toward purchasing the property

## 1991

Huge "For Sale" sign posted by BN subsidiary Glacier Park

SCLP publishes PR booklet and coordinates press coverage to secure state funding

*Minneapolis Star Tribune* endorses acquisition of Cedar Lake Park

Hedberg Family Foundation pledges $200,000 toward trail development

Audubon Chapter of Minneapolis donates $15,000 sanctuary fund to help purchase land

St. Louis Park High School group "Save Our Surroundings" donates proceeds from Bowlathon

Audubon selects SCLP to receive funds raised from Birdathon

Benefit Concert by local musicians raises $9,000 for SCLP

SCLP receives CUE (Committee on Urban Environment) Award

Minnesota Legislature approves $1.2 million for acquiring land

SCLP presents MPRB with check for $487,000 in private funds toward purchase of land

James Ford Bell Foundation awards $5,000 grant and interest-free loan for purchase

On November 25, MPRB purchases 48 acres of land north of Cedar Lake

## 1992

MPRB and SCLP form Partnership to continue park and trail development

MPRB unveils concept design for Cedar Lake Regional Trail

MPRB, SCLP, and Sierra Club submit proposal for trail development to state legislature

MPLS Public Works (MPW) joins Partnership to develop Cedar Lake Regional Trail

*CLPA Update* article reports on antics of Cedar Lake Park "fox family"

MPRB and SCLP sponsor Land Acquisition Celebration on July 26

Minnesota Volkssports Association sponsors Walk & Roll for Cedar Lake Park

MPRB convenes Cedar Lake Park & Trails Citizens' Advisory Committee

MnDOT applies for federal funds for Cedar Lake Regional Trail construction

Hedberg Family Foundation pledges $200,000 toward Cedar Lake Regional Trail

Legislature awards Partnership $610,000 for Cedar Lake Regional Trail

Seventeen eastern bluebirds hatch and fledge in the park

SCLP sponsors Cedar Lake Park Clean-Up Days with Sierra Club and MPRB

Audubon builds osprey nesting platform alongside Cedar Lake

SCLP proposes Cedar Grove Memorial in the park

## 1993

SCLP receives North Star State Bicycle Award for trail initiative

Cedar Lake Park & Trails CAC completes Statement of Philosophy and Design Principles

Partnership seeks proposals from landscape architects to design park and trail

Partnership selects Jones & Jones/Richard Haag Associates to design park and trail

SCLP participates in Earth Walk '93

MPRB conducts Water Quality Management Study which includes Cedar Lake

Northern States Power runs 75 public service messages thanking SCLP for their efforts to save Cedar Lake Park

Jones & Jones completes schematic trail design

MPW receives $500,000 in federal ISTEA funds for Cedar Lake Regional Trail

### 1994

Save Cedar Lake Park (SCLP) becomes Cedar Lake Park Association (CLPA)

DNR distributes CLPA's Organizational Guidelines to user groups across the state

CLPA hosts Third Annual Osprey Release

Audubon reports four successful nestings in bluebird boxes

MPRB unveils plan to recreate wetlands at southwest corner of Cedar Lake

Cellular One works with Partnership to create Linden Yard Station

Federal Highway Administration (FHWA) approves funding to complete Cedar Lake Regional Trail

Third annual Earth Day clean-up of park

### 1995

CLPA unveils 100–Year Vision for Cedar Lake

CLPA and MPRB convene workshop to educate public on buckthorn

Audubon sights mallards, Canadian geese, and wood ducks

Partnership breaks ground on Cedar Lake Regional Trail on February 17

"Bulldozers in the Sanctuary" contours park and constructs trail

Prairie Restorations, Inc., seeds Cedar Lake Prairie with native plants.

Partnership receives FHWA's First Annual Environmental Award in Washington D.C.

CLPA commissions a history of the Cedar Lake Park Association

MPRB's "Team Teamwork" crew removes tons of debris from north shore of lake

DNR awards $10,000 grant to CLPA for native plant community restoration

CLPA proposes restoring maple-basswood forest along lake's northeast shoreline

Cedar Lake Regional Trail opens with festive celebration on September 9

Greater Kenwood Botanical Society initiates Wildflower Demonstration Plot

CLPA hosts National Recreation & Parks Association workshop

Researcher interviews founders for Cedar Lake Park Association history project

## 1996

Kenwood-Isles Area Association (KIAA) allocates $95,000 for 21st & Upton improvement

Chain of Lakes comprehensive planning process begins

Audubon members initiate Birding Day in Cedar Lake Park

DNR approves maple-basswood Big Woods Restoration Project

Wood chipping begins on lake's north shore

MPRB builds CLPA-funded bench near Hedberg Donation Rock in prairie

CLPA participates in Kenilworth Trail Citizens' Advisory Committee

First prairie mowing by MPRB

MPRB treats lake with aluminum sulfate to help restore water quality

Drum and song ceremony dedicates Cedar Lake Park Memorial Grove on October 6

**1997**

CLPA members participate in Midtown Greenway Development along 29th Street corridor

Audubon spots over 129 species of birds in park including the common egret

CLPA hosts lecture by local historian Deborah Morse-Kahn on Henry Thoreau's walk through Cedar Lake area

St. David's Society, People for Parks, and CLPA plant 1,200 daffodils on south shore

Audubon sights Caspian terns, black-crowned night herons, and whip-poor-wills

CLPA presents Cedar Lake Park Concept Master Plan to MPRB

*CLPA Update* newsletter masthead changes from "Save Cedar Lake Park" to "Cedar Lake Park Association" indicating shift from saving to sustaining the park

Birder identifies whistling swan at Cedar Lake

MPRB completes Cedar Meadows Wetlands Project at southwest corner of lake

**1998**

Former president of SCLP heads group to develop Bassett's Creek Corridor

First CLPA-sponsored Wildflower Planting in the Cedar Lake Park prairie

CLPA plants bur oak in prairie to honor MPRB Environmentalist Al Singer

CLPA speaks to Minneapolis Hiking Club and Hennepin County Extension Service

Water quality improves in Cedar Lake

DNR provides $10,000 grant to complete Big Woods I

Summer storm batters lakeshore, knocking down trees and temporarily closing trail

Citizens' Advisory Committee convenes to study dog issues in city parks

Dunwoody students and faculty help design Cedar Grove double spiral

Volunteers plant sixty more trees in Cedar Grove

St. Paul Highland Jr. High volunteers spend "Make a Difference Day" planting in the park

Rail traffic returns to the Kenilworth Corridor

DNR approves funding for Big Woods II

Kenilworth Trail construction begins in November

### 1999

City announces plans to replace eighty-three-year-old Cedar Lake Parkway Bridge

MPW and MPRB invite CLPA to participate in Cedar Lake Parkway Bridge CAC

KIAA uses Neighborhood Revitalization Program funds to enhance 21st & Upton Gateway

Boy Scouts and other volunteers participate in 2nd Wildflower Prairie Planting

CLPA member survey prioritizes trails, connections, and security in the park

Cash on Plus and Twin Cities Tree Trust plant trees along northwest shore

HCRRA completes Kenilworth Trail

### 2000

MPW proposes on-road alignment to complete Cedar Lake Regional Trail to the river

CLPA advocates off-road alignment of trail to the river as planned in 1989 Wirth Study

Midtown Greenway construction begins

KIAA completes 21st & Upton Prairie Native-Species Restoration

Big Woods II project to plant eighteen species of hedges and shrubs alongside prairie

Midtown Greenway opens with segment connecting to Kenilworth Trail

Wood chipping of trails begins along north shore of lake

CLPA oversees design of Linda Jadwin Memorial

## 2001

HCRRA completes Hutch Spur between Cedar Lake Regional Trail and Hopkins Depot

CLPA funds study to confirm feasibility of off-road alignment of trail to the river

Completion of Hutch Spur creates 12-mile Cedar Lake Loop with Cedar Lake Regional Trail, Kenilworth Trail, Midtown Greenway, and Cedar Lake LRT Trail

Ceremony marks completion of Linda Jadwin Memorial near Hidden Beach

CLPA and MPRB fund water pump in Cedar Lake Park Prairie

Volunteers design historical panels for new Cedar Lake Parkway Bridge

## 2002

Data Recognition Corporation (DRC) employees participate in wildflower planting

CLPA pitches off-road trail alignment to MPLS City Council Member Lisa Goodman

CLPA launches website

Bassett's Creek (Luce Line) Trail links to Cedar Lake Regional Trail

CLPA meets with State Representative Margaret Anderson Kelliher to advocate off-road alignment of trail to the river

CLPA confers with Burlington Northern concerning trail to the river

## 2003

CLPA serves refreshments on Lake of the Isles at inaugural City of
Lakes Loppet Ski Race

Ice out on lake April 3

"Help Finish Cedar Lake Regional Trail to the Mississippi River"
signs appear in park

CLPA meets with Congressman Martin Sabo about preferred alignment of trail to the river

Long-delayed work begins to replace Cedar Lake Parkway Bridge

CLPA members discuss preferred alignment with Congressman Jim
Oberstar while biking the Cedar Lake Regional Trail

CLPA participates in Bryn Mawr Music Festival

## 2004

CLPA serves refreshments at 2nd Loppet

Prairie/Woodland Restoration gets underway along the Kenilworth
Trail

CLPA gains congressional support for preferred alignment of trail
to the river

Member funds installation of Cedar Lake Park Memorial Grove
Bench

Audubon sights songbirds, loons, and mature bald eagle at Cedar
Lake

Audubon conducts Christmas bird count

## 2005

Loppet canceled due to lack of snow

Ice out on lake April 5

MPRB conducts spring prairie burning in Cedar Lake Park

Cedar Lake Prairie Plant Transect Survey catalogs plant life in
prairie

Two pairs of eastern bluebirds nesting in the Cedar Lake Park Prairie

Burnham Uplands Demonstration Project begins removing buckthorn and other exotics

CLPA celebrates the opening of the third Cedar Lake Parkway Bridge

Bridge panels created by CLPA volunteers commemorate history of
Cedar Lake area

Federal Transportation Act provides additional funding for trail to
the river


### 2006

CLPA becomes a sponsor of revived Loppet Ski Race

Ice out on lake April 7

CLPA honored with Fitness Minnesota Award

St. Louis Park constructs access ramp to Cedar Lake Regional Trail

Burnham Uplands Demonstration Project clears large stretch of
buckthorn


### 2007

CLPA provides refreshments at Loppet Ski Race

Theodore Wirth III speaks at CLPA Annual Meeting

Ice out on lake March 27

Audubon reports eagles, loons, and warblers at lake during spring

CLPA commissions Cedar Lake Park Concept Mound Plan

CLPA meets with city engineers on completing trail to the river


### 2008

CLPA and Providence Academy volunteers provide soup for Loppet

CLPA develops Southwest LRT Policy and Design Principles

CLPA participates in Hennepin County's Southwest LRT Advisory
Committee

Burnham Uplands Demonstration Project reintroduces native
flora

Yale alumni volunteers work on Burnham Uplands Project

City counts 1,200 riders a day at the Cedar Lake & Kenilworth Trail junction

MPRB designates the informally known "Hidden Beach" as "East Cedar Lake Beach"

## 2009

CLPA and Providence Academy volunteers staff food tent for Loppet in February

Ice out on lake April 4

CLPA celebrates its twenty-year anniversary under the Cedar Lake Parkway Bridge

Burnham Uplands Demonstration Project reintroduces oaks, cedars, and sumac

Hennepin County Regional Railroad Authority chooses Kenilworth for Southwest LRT route

Audubon reports sightings of Cooper's hawks, herons and egrets, loons, and songbirds

CLPA members meet with county staff to define mowing area along Kenilworth Trail

City extends Cedar Lake Regional Trail–Royalston Trailhead to Target Field

CLPA board approves new budget for Cedar Lake Park Association history project

## 2010

MPRB and CLPA meet in January to initiate new Adopt-A-Park policy

CLPA and Providence Academy provide hot soup for cold Loppet racers in February

Ice out on lake March 29

Minneapolis City Council approves award of trail construction contract on May 28

CLPA participates in the MPRB Southwest LRT Citizens' Advisory Committee

Construction of trail to the river begins in downtown Minneapolis in September

CLPA sponsors Southwest LRT Design Charrette in October

CLPA distributes Southwest LRT Design Principles for Cedar Lake to decision-makers

## 2011

Ice out on lake April 10

CLPA serves refreshments at Loppet in February

Ribbon cutting opens Cedar Lake Regional Trail to Mississippi River on May 14

DRC employees plant wildflowers in the park for the tenth consecutive year

MPW performs patching and crack sealing on old section of trail

CLPA receives $7,000 award from Minnesota Historical and Cultural Grant to publish *Cedar Lake Park Association: A History*

# Appendix D.
## SCLP/CLPA LEADERSHIP, 1989–2011

**Save Cedar Lake Park**
**Founding Board of Directors: 1989**

President Brian Willette
Vice President Elly Sturgis
Secretary/Treasurer Doris Peterson
Dan Dailey

**SCLP/CLPA Presidents: 1989–2011**

Brian Willette
Dan Dailey
Keith Prussing

**SCLP/CLPA Board Members: 1989–2011**

| | | |
|---|---|---|
| Don Beimborn | David Klopp | Keith Prussing |
| Mary Conway | Laurie Lundy | Steni Prussing |
| Dan Dailey | Wally Marx | George Puzak |
| Bob Day | Stacy McMahon | John Richter |
| David Dayton | Jim McPherson | Dorene Scriven |
| Frank Dorsal | Meredith | Jeanette Sobania |
| Steve Durrant | Montgomery | Dan Steinberg |
| Ned Foster | Sarah Mushlitz | Elly Sturgis |
| John Herman | John Perentesis | D'Ann Topoluk |
| Linda Huhn | Doris Peterson | Neil Trembley |
| Ruth Jones | Jim Preston | Brian Willette |

# Appendix E. Species Recorded in 2011 Prairie Survey

SPECIES RECORDED IN SUMMER 2011

IN THE CEDAR LAKE PARK PRAIRIE

*Relative abundance based on percent, cover, and frequency of occurrence*

## A = Abundant  C =Common  U = Uncommon  R = Rare

| Species | Relative Abundance | Native/ Alien |
|---|---|---|
| Big Bluestem  *Andropogon gerardi* | A | N |
| Common Ragweed  *Ambrosia artemisiifolia* | A | N |
| Switch Grass  *Panicum virgatum* | A | N |
| Wild Bergamot  *Monarda fistulosa* | A | N |
| Aster sp.  *Asteraceae* | C | N |
| Black Medick  *Medicago lupulina* | C | A |
| Black-Eyed Susan  *Rudbeckia hirta* | C | N |
| Brome Grass  *Bromus ciliatus* | C | N |
| Canada Wild Rye  *Elymus canadensis* | C | N |
| Common Cinquefoil  *Potentilla simplex* | C | N |
| Common Mullein  *Verbascum thapsus* | C | A |
| Common Plantain  *Plantago major* | C | A |
| Field Bindweed  *Convolvulus arvensis* | C | A |
| Gumweed  *Grindelia squarrosa* | C | N |
| Hoary Alyssum  *Berteroa incana* | C | A |
| Hoary Vervain  *Verbena stricta* | C | N |
| Leafy Spurge  *Euphorbia esula* | C | A |
| Little Bluestem  *Andropogn scoparius* | A | N |
| Prairie Clover spp.  *Petalostemum* | A | N |
| Round-Headed Bush Clover  *Lespedeza capitata* | C | N |
| Side-Oats Gramma  *Bouteloua curtipendula* | A | N |

| Species | Relative Abundance | Native/ Alien |
|---|---|---|
| Spotted Knapweed  *Centaurea maculosa* | C | A |
| Sweet Clover sp.  *Melilotus* | C | A |
| Unidentified member of Pea Family  *Leguminosae* | U | |
| White Sage  *Artemesia ludoviciana* | C | N |
| White Sweet Clover  *Melilotus alba* | C | A |
| Box Elder  *Acer negundo* | R | N |
| Butterfly Milkweed  *Asclepias tuberosa* | R | N |
| Curly Dock  *Rumex crispus* | R | A |
| Elm spp.  *Ulmus* | R | |
| Gray-Headed Coneflower  *Ratibida pinnata* | R | N |
| Green-Headed Coneflower  *Rudbeckia laciniata* | R | N |
| Rough Blazing Star  *Liatris aspera* | R | N |
| Whorled Milkweed  *Asclepias verticillata* | R | N |
| Yarrow  *Achillea millefolium* | R | N |
| Bladder Campion  *Silene dichotoma* | U | A |
| Canada Goldenrod  *Solidago canadensis* | C | N |
| Catnip  *Nepeta cataria* | U | A |
| Common Dandelion  *Taraxacum officinale* | U | N |
| Hairy Grama Grass  *Bouteloua hirsuta* | U | N |
| Horseweed  *Erigeron canadensis* | U | N |
| Indian Grass  *Sorghastrum nutans* | A | N |
| Lamb's Quarters  *Chenopodium album* | U | A |
| Lead Plant  *Amorpha canescens* | C | N |
| Mint spp.  *Labiatae* | U | N |
| Partridge Pea  *Chamaecrista fasciculata* | C | N |
| Rigid Goldenrod  *Solidago rigida* | U | N |
| Sumac species  *Rhus* | U | N |
| Evening primrose  *Onagraceae biennis* | U | N |
| Prairie Cord Gras  *Spartina pectinata* | U | N |
| Willow spp.  *Salix* | U | N |
| Aspen spp.  *Populus* | U | N |

# Credits

**This book is the product of efforts of many CLPA members**

Frederick Appell  
Jan Borene  
Chris Carlson  
Steve Durrant  
John Finn  
Heidi (Adelheid) Fischer  
Bob Glancy  

Stacy McMahon  
Jim McPherson  
Meredith Montgomery  
Keith Prussing  
Joseph Schmitz  
D'Ann Topoluk  
Brian Willette  

**CLPA would like to thank the staff**
**of the following collections for their support**

Minneapolis Collection, James K. Hosmer Special Collections, Hennepin County Public Library, Minnesota Historical Society

**CLPA would also like to thank**

Deborah Morse-Kahn, Marilyn Ziebarth, and David C. Smith for critiquing the text and suggesting the addition of sections concerning the history of land use in the area and the growth of the prairie.

Judy Gilats for book design and production.

Christine Pistulka for editing.

Zan Ceeley for proofreading.

Meredith Montgomery for use of her photographs on pages 12, 30, 66, and 83 and as credited.

Dorothy Childers for use of her photographs.

Don Beimborn for use of his photograph.

# Oral History and Notes

AN INVALUABLE PRIMARY RESOURCE WAS OBTAINED IN THE ORAL histories conducted to benefit the CLPA in its desire to record and document the contributions and memories of citizen participants, agency representatives, and area residents of neighborhoods bordering the park. These interviews provided the quotations found throughout this publication.

## Interviews by Adelheid Fisher

Dan Dailey, interview by Adelheid Fisher, Minneapolis, MN, fall 1995.

John Herman, interview by Adelheid Fisher, Minneapolis, MN, fall 1995.

Laurie Lundy, interview by Adelheid Fisher, Minneapolis, MN, fall 1995.

Corwin Peterson, interview by Adelheid Fisher, Minneapolis, MN, fall 1995.

Keith Prussing, interview by Adelheid Fisher, Minneapolis, MN, fall 1995.

John Richter, interview by Adelheid Fisher, Minneapolis, MN, fall 1995.

Brian Willette, interview by Adelheid Fisher, Minneapolis, MN, fall 1995.

## Interviews by Neil Trembley

Ruth Jones, interview by Neil Trembley, Minneapolis, MN, June 30, 1992.

Laurie Lundy, interview by Neil Trembley, Minneapolis, MN, November 9, 1997.

George Puzak, interview by Neil Trembley, Minneapolis, MN, July 7, 1999.

Louis Claussen, interview by Neil Trembley, Minneapolis, MN, April 4, 2000.

Billy Binder, interview by Neil Trembley, Minneapolis, MN, September 17, 2007.

John Richter, interview by Neil Trembley, Minneapolis, MN, May 21, 2010.

Jack Yuzna, email message to Neil Trembley, September 29, 2011.

## Notes

1. "President Wilber F. Decker's Explanatory Sketch of the Pre-Glacial Course of the Mississippi River in his Annual Report of 1909 on Pages 9 to 13," in Theodore Wirth, *Minneapolis Park System: 1883–1944* (Minneapolis: Minneapolis Parks Legacy Society, 2006), 80.

2. Isaac Atwater, *History of the City of Minneapolis, Minnesota* (New York: Munsell & Co., 1893), 18–19.

3. David Lanagren and Ernest Sandeen, *The Lake District of Minneapolis: A History of the Calhoun-Isles Community* (Minneapolis: University of Minnesota Press, 2004), 5–11.

4. Lanagren, *The Lake District of Minneapolis*, 11.

5. Jesse T. Jarrett, *U.S. Surveyor General Survey Notes and Field Notes, 1853*. Box 5.57.J6.3B, R24 T29 Sec. 29-32v, Minnesota Historical Society. Minnesota History Center, St. Paul.

6. Theodore Wirth, *Minneapolis Park System: 1883–1944* (Minneapolis: Minneapolis Parks Legacy Society, 2006), 96.

7. David C. Smith, *Parks, Lakes, Trails and So Much More: An Overview of the Histories of MPRB Properties* (Minneapolis Parks and Recreation Board, 2008), 27. http://www.minneapolisparks.org/documents/parks/Parks_Lakes_Trails_Much_More.pdf (accessed June 12, 2012).

8. George Rice, "Progress Misses Cedar Lake and Years Dim Colorful Past," *Minneapolis Star*, July 7, 1952.

9. James T. Wold, "An Historic Look at the Minneapolis & St. Louis Railroad," *Lake Area News*, June 1993, 38–42.

10. Horace W. S. Cleveland, "Suggestions for a System of Parks and Parkways

for the City of Minneapolis," in Theodore Wirth, *Minneapolis Park System: 1883–1944* (Minneapolis: Minneapolis Parks Legacy Society, 2006), 28–34.

11. Theodore Wirth, *Minneapolis Park System*, 113–166.

12. "Excerpt from a Thank You Letter from the DNR." *Save Cedar Lake Park Update*, Spring 1994, 4.

13. Wirth Design Associates, *Concept Master Plan for a Potential Connection of Wirth Regional Park, Chain of Lakes Regional Park and the Central Regional Park by use of the Existing Railroad Corridor, Prepared for: The Minneapolis Park Board*, Billings: 1989.

14. *Save Cedar Lake Park Booklet*. Minneapolis: Mar. 1991, 1–15.

15. J. A. Mayor, letter to C.H. Warren, May 6, 1889. *Great Northern Records*. Right of Way & Plat Books of StPM&M.

16. *Great Northern Records*. Bridge Records,138.J.9.38 Box 1Folder 9: 5. Minnesota Historical Society, Minnesota History Center, St. Paul.

17. Minneapolis City Council Standing Committee On Roads & Bridges, letter to Great Northern. July 9, 1915, *Great Northern Records*. President's List, 133.I.9.10 (F) Folder 6756. Minnesota Historical Society, Minnesota History Center, St. Paul.

18. Greg Brown and Anthony Wagner, *Cedar Lake Regional Trail Alternative Alignment, Washington Avenue to West River Road: A Summary Report*. Sept. 2002, CLPA Archive. Excerpts from the Summary, *CLPA Update*, Winter 2003, 3.

19. Scott Russell, "Downtown needs complicate lakes to the river 'bike highway.'" *Downtown Journal*. March 3, 2003.

20. *Request for City Council Committee Action, From the Department of Public Works, Subject: Cedar Lake Trail Phase III, Dec. 12, 2006*. http://www.minneapolismn.gov/www/groups/public/@council/documents/webcontent/convert_260875.pdf (accessed July 26, 2012).

21. Neil Trembley, "The Cedar Lake Trail to the Mississippi," *Bryn Mawr Bugle*, June 2011.

22. "The Dream Comes to Pass: Ribbon-cutting Marks Completion of the Trail to the River," *Hill & Lake Press*, June, 17, 2011.

# Bibliography

THE MOST CRITICAL MATERIALS DOCUMENTING THE SCLP/CLPA are the association newsletters (1990–present) and the association archives (letters, flyers, minutes, planning maps).

Other sources used as background information for the writing of this book include are listed below.

Atwater, Isaac. *History of Minneapolis Minnesota.* 2 vols. New York: Munsell & Co., 1893.

Brown, Greg, and Anthony Wagner. *Cedar Lake Regional Trail Alternative Alignment, Washington Avenue to West River Road: A Summary Report.* Minneapolis: 2002.

Cedar Lake Park Preservation and Development Association. *Save Cedar Lake Park Booklet.* Minneapolis: 1991.

Cleveland, Horace W. S. "Suggestions for a System of Parks and Parkways for the City of Minneapolis." In Theodore Wirth, *Minneapolis Park System: 1883–1944.* 1948. Minneapolis: Minneapolis Parks Legacy Society, 2006.

Decker, Wilber F. "Explanatory Sketch of the Pre-Glacial Course of the Mississippi River in his Annual Report of 1909." In Theodore Wirth, *Minneapolis Park System: 1883–1944.* 1948. Minneapolis: Minneapolis Parks Legacy Society, 2006.

Folwell, William W., ed. *A History of Minnesota.* Vol. III, 1926. St. Paul: Minnesota Historical Society, 1969.

Jarrett, Jesse, T., *U.S. Surveyor General Survey Notes and Field Notes 1853,* Box 5.57.J6.3B, R24 T29 Sec. 29-32v, Minnesota Historical Society, Minnesota History Center, St. Paul.

Lanegran, David, and Ernest Sandeen. *The Lake District of Minneapolis: A History of the Calhoun-Isles Community.* Minneapolis: University of Minnesota P, 2004.

Smith, David C. *City of Parks: The Story of Minneapolis Parks.* The Foundation for Minneapolis Parks: 2008.

Wallof, William. *Wallof Photograph Collection: 1890–1918.* Minneapolis Collection, James K. Hosmer Special Collections Library, Hennepin County Library, Minneapolis, Minnesota.

Wirth Design Associates, *Concept Master Plan for a Potential Connection of Wirth Regional Park, Chain of Lakes Regional Park and the Central Regional Park by use of the Existing Railroad Corridor, Prepared for: The Minneapolis Park Board.* Billings, Montana: 1989.

Wirth, Theodore. *Minneapolis Park System: 1883–1944.* 1948. Minneapolis: Minneapolis Parks Legacy Society, 2006.

# Index